DO YOU REALLY WANNA KNOW?

Kristin N. Howard

Copyright © 2017 Kristin Howard

All rights reserved.

ISBN:0692091955
ISBN-13: 978-0692091951

This book is dedicated to all the young girls, ladies, and women out there who weren't fortunate enough to make it out the game without a criminal record or alive for that matter. You're the reason I speak out, the reason God has given me strength, and the reason I know I have been granted everlasting grace and mercy. In sharing my story, I have received a healing that only HE can provide. I used to be you. Your future is much brighter than anything money can buy. There is a way out, I'm out so, WE OUT! ***I AM MY SISTERS.***

CONTENTS

	Acknowledgments	I
	Lights	
1	Humble Beginnings	Pg#8
2	When Just Observing	Pg. #11
	He Shared Her	
3	My Rome'	Pg. #18
	Black Sheep	
4	Life on The Other Side of the Diploma	Pg. #26
	Sin's Way	
5	Meeting Sin	Pg. #31
	Untitled	
6	It's Complicated	Pg. #35
	Redemption	
7	No New Friends	Pg. #41
	Unexpected	
8	"E"mpty Purse	Pg. #51
	Flawed	
9	First of Three	Pg. #56
	Corruptor	
10	Online Shenanigans	Pg. #62
	Hard Nights	
11	Second of Three	Pg. #69
	HOE$	
12	Its All Good Until It's Not	Pg. #77
	Love Me My Love	
13	Third of Three	Pg. #91

Acknowledgments:

THE MOST HIGH IS REAL! God, I praise you, I thank you every day for your grace and mercy. I'm grateful for this opportunity that you've blessed me with to be a blessing to those in need of your love. Thank you Lord for keeping me under your wing. To my family, you've known and supported the telling of my journey to the world for the greater good, thank you. My parents, K.J. and Liz, I love you both. It's because of your prayers and love for me that I live today. For the many nights, you had to come and get me from my apartment and the nights you stayed up with my son. I'm forever indebted to you both. The world's most amazing siblings; Kenny Jr., Kyle, Kris, and Kaila. The secrets we have, the fights we've had, and the future that God has in store for us is great. We're Howards, I love you all and appreciate everything you do. To my son, Logan Love you are the best thing that has ever happened to Mommy. You've been rockin' with me the whole way and I promise you it's not in vain. Everything I do, I do it for you. You deserve the best because that's all you've given me. To my son's dad, my ex-pimp/boyfriend and to all the others thank you. I love and forgive you, so does Christ. Jshauntae Marshall, my sister, my friend, my "GO FOR IT BABYGIRL, I GOT'CHA BACK", I love you. To my day ones Bri, Dessy and "J" all of you knew somebody had to tell it, why not me? Thank you, my loves. My friend and DOLL HOUSE Stylist, Sandra I love you girl, I heard you and I got us, forward and upward!

To my readers, thank you for supporting my movement, this is my life, an open book. Your interest and curiosity is raising awareness about a lifestyle that is glorified for all the wrong reasons. There will always be a short cut to anything you want to accomplish in life, but the price you pay for not investing that extra time may cost your LIFE! Let's build a LEGACY! Slow motion is ALWAYS better than no motion. Peace.

LIGHTS

Las Vegas life is very cool,

But not a lot of girls stay in school.

There's a lot of casinos,

So, a lot of people hope to win playing BINGO.

A lot of lights,

Which is tight and bright.

There are a lot of churches on the West part of town,

But, not a lot of people that go.

If they do it's just to put on a show.

A lot of family live out here,

A lot more drama.

Oooh, DEAR!

You must be 18-21 to do a lot of things,

Except sing and hear the school 2:11 bell ring.

It's been cool living out here,

Because this is where I got my ears pierced.

By: K. Nicole Howard (April 2nd, 2003)

HUMBLE BEGININGS

There I was, again. Sitting on the King size bed, in my hotel room, near the beautiful Leadbetter Beach of Santa Barbara, California. Disgusted, confused, and at best, all out baffled at the fact that he could even fix his mouth to speak to me like that. It's been over three years since we've been rockin' and he's going to take the side of this little girl while he's in Texas doing only God knows what. If it were left up to me, I'd be solo, like it's been. Not missing a single beat or dollar that was ever printed. Yet, I'm the one stuck doing on-the-go hoe training. Two Hispanics teenagers, eighteen and nineteen years old… at least that's how old I thought they were. I guess now would be a good time to introduce myself.

Kristin Nicole Howard is my government name but I've worked under many. Mia, Redd, SweetCheekz to name a few. Born to Kenneth and Elizabeth Howard, of Chicago, Illinois. My father; a Marine and Pastor. My Mom; a wife, worker, and great homemaker. They raised me along with four of the world's greatest human beings. My three brothers; Kenny Jr. "Oldest", Kyle "Squirly", Kris "Budge" and my younger sister Kaila "Bubbles". We grew up going to church and often being called "PK's", short for preachers' kids. Growing up, we would hear people say PK's were the worst but never knew why or understood what that meant. Let's just say as I got older, it wasn't long before I saw why it was so commonly said that "PK's were the worst".

For the most part, my childhood was amazing! My family and I didn't have the fancy cars and clothes. We didn't have big nice houses that Pastors usually have or any of the materialistic things. We had each other. Whatever one went through, we all went through as a family. I remember having friends that would call us lucky because our parents were still together instead of divorced. Little did they know it was the furthest thing from luck some days. Two working parents in the home and as children having to attend church regularly, we weren't exposed to a lot of things. It's safe to say that our parents did a great job at sheltering us from the difficulties of life.

Being the only girl for the first ten years wasn't easy but it sure had its perks! My brothers always teased me about my Dad having the "Baby Girl" syndrome. His punishments and whooping's being harder on them then they would ever be on me. Don't get it twisted though, my Mom got me for every single time my Dad didn't.

There were almost always people at our house, enjoying our home, where ever that may have been. Church members, family, friends, we even had a foster brother named Ruben. He was taken away from us by his biological family while we were still young and living in Arizona. That's the first time I ever remember feeling my heart hurt in the most abnormal way. From Arizona we moved to Nevada, where my life began to take many unfathomable turns.

We moved to Las Vegas when I was ten years old. From the ages of ten to about fifteen we moved quite a bit. As a young teenage girl growing up in Las Vegas, life was exciting but horrible at the same time. It's like being a child on a playground full of exciting new things to do but still needing your parents support to enjoy them. More times than not I was the youngest in the circle that I hung out with or my parents weren't having it which didn't allow me many options. With both of my parents working full time jobs while serving the ministry at church, you can believe all five us found ways to occupy our time. I found my love in reading, writing, and dancing all around the same time. We would ride the bus to the library some days and because I hung out with people at least 7-10 years older than me I knew very well about Eric Jerome Dickey, Zane, and Tracy Brown. It was the erotica, gangster love books that sparked my interest in story telling through writing. Once my Mom picked up *G- Spot* by Noire off my bed she banded all books of that genre from her home. Being true to self, yes, I began to sneak them in and finish them out before she knew anything about them. This is where the "game" began for me. I wanted to live the life of the main female character in the books I'd been reading.

What you think, you create. What you feel, you attract. What you imagine, you BECOME!

The young ladies in the books that run into the drug king pin, the club owner/boss, or mafia guys living the life of luxury, made a way to also experience the finer things in life… with them. They intrigued me and kept my full, undivided attention for the entire 2-3 days it took me to finish the book.

At the age of 17, I was introduced to many different females. Little did I know, each of them would help me to become what they called a "solid bottom bitch". She is the one girl the pimp or nigga reserves for himself, or also respected as the player's favorite girl. The one that regardless of what he may do, say or dream about it was her job and her job only to make sure those things happened. That his dreams came to life.

WHEN JUST OBSERVING.

The first young lady I ran into I'll never forget. I was a junior in high school and her name was Vida. She always had a car, all the latest and greatest name brand clothes. Vida had a guy that would give her whatever she wanted whenever she wanted it. She met these guys off a telephone chat line. You make an introduction of yourself in your sexiest, most seductive voice and they'd respond back based on if you said anything they liked to hear. One day after school I asked my Mom if it was okay if I went to her house. Of course, she said yes because the motive was to get our homework done. That day she taught me how and what to say to get the things I wanted. I began to use it regularly and check my messages every other day. Most of them, full of crap but this one seemed so sincere and sweet. His name was Core. He was 5'7" tall, 32 years old single man who lived alone drove a nice car and worked an honest job. He pretty much had everything I needed to use to my advantage. We exchanged phone numbers and began to see one another on a regular basis without my parents knowing. No, I wasn't allowed to be out late night, let alone spend the night with a 32-year-old at his apartment. He worked as a lead manager over at the Chevrolet and drove a Cadillac Deville that I had most of the time while he was at work.

Core was a sweet guy but only seemed to be looking for love. He wanted to be intimate *all* the time. Affectionate to his very core. Anything I'd ask for he'd give it to me until one day he came home from work and said, "I give you everything but now it's time for you to return the favor or we're done, I'm cutting you off." That was it, the first time I had ever laid with a man for "things". This became our regular routine after about 4 months. Let me remind you, I was still on the chat line and wanted to make sure I had a good roster before I just cut Core off clean. So, when I successfully had another runner up, Core came home from work and I let him know my things were packed up in the car and he could drop me off at home, we were done.

He cried, begged and pleaded with me to not let this so called "amazing chemistry" we had go. He even went as far as telling me he would kill himself. We remained friends for a few months afterwards… that was until one day while talking on the phone and my Mom picked up and heard our conversation. She immediately told me, "Your father and I need to meet this Core guy or you will be on punishment for eternity."

A few days had gone by and I had arranged the meeting. I knew it was a wrap when they saw the Cadillac pull up front. My father went down stairs to speak with him and I never heard from Core after that ever again.

It didn't really bother me but it threw me off because now I would be under parental surveillance because of someone I had already cut ties with anyway. None of that mattered to me because I still had a plan. Growing up I was involved in various dance groups, made money baby sitting and had one or two other outlets that knew about my desire to get out of the house and do me. Like the saying goes, "My parents raised me right, I did wrong on my own". That was me! To get out the house, I would use the positive people in my life that my parents wouldn't mind me staying overnight with.

I was in a Christian dance group called the Tribe of Judah. There I met a lady we called, "P". She was such a sweet lady. P was married, loved me and my family, but she had just had weight loss surgery and wanted to live the fast life and be young again. We shared clothes, I packed two bags when going to her house. One bag contained clothes for dance practice and the other containing clothing to get into this little hole in the wall spot called, Seven Seas on Lake Mead and J Street. We would go out kick it with different guys, smoke, drink and live it up. At least for the night. She was into the internet and introduced me to a website called Tagged and MocoSpace. It wasn't really my thing because I'm a face value kind of girl. However, I found the internet useful to brush up on my game, word play. Surprisingly I found out that you could be whomever you wanted to be online.

I began meeting guys who had cars, money, and material things. All of those things benefited me. If he didn't have anything material or monetary to offer, he didn't know me. He couldn't cross this bridge unless he could pay the toll.

We introduced ourselves to guys as sisters, me of course being the younger one and from what I was told the prettier one. I was on my way to her house on the public transportation bus and when I got off at the corner of Gowan and Martin Luther King there is this beautiful white DENALI truck with 26 inch rims waiting for me. The man inside said he saw me when I got on at Lake Mead but I hadn't paying him any attention.

He asked if he could talk to me for a second and I said, "For what, about what?" He was very persistent in his pursuit which to me was amusing yet flattering.

I had considered myself to be simply the girl next door who had a ton of brothers and a crazy father with many, many, many guns! Because I didn't have a cell phone at the time he gave me his number and we began to chop it up from time to time. His name was Rome. He was 29 years old and lived in a studio apartment aside his grandparents' house near The View.

The house was a pretty decent size. There was a door that connected his bathroom to the main part of the house. He said his grandparents were all he had and he would never just leave them to live by themselves. This type of living arrangement helped him as well while he was working, going to school, and saving his money. "The View" was a street called Valley View off the west side of Las Vegas where all the hood niggas, d-boys and gang bangers kicked it or trapped at. Most of them like Rome had grew up there and trapped over in those neighborhoods for the longest. Rome wasn't into that type of thing though. He worked construction by day and went to welding/foundation laying school by night. He was about 6'2, smooth, chocolate skin that laid over his decent body. He kept his hair shoulder length typically braided…sometimes beaded at the end. One of my favorite things about him was the hair on his face. His goatee was perfection and I loved it! We would talk on the phone for hours but mostly we talked over the weekends.

He turned in early during the week due to me having to catch the city bus to school at 6am and him having to be at work by 5am. It was my parents, my younger sister, her cat Chloe my youngest brother and my twin living in the Budget Suites off Lake Mead and Rancho at the time. That was a really difficult time in our lives but my Dad promised my Mom that we would not have to go back and live with my grandmother. He did everything in his power to keep that promise and he did.

So, it was a little hard to get privacy and sneak the phone in the room to talk to Rome but I made it happen. After a few weeks, he began to meet me in the back of the suites just to see me. We would sit in his truck for minutes that seemed like hours talking about everything under the sun. He was a genuine kind of guy.

He was always interested in what I had to say, how I was feeling, how I was doing in school and what I had planned after I finished.

He had everything a young and very impressionable girl could ask for. When I didn't feel good, he would bring me things. There were times he would even bring me flowers and cards just to say he was thinking of me.

As the end of my junior year of high school was ending I remember him telling me he was taking a cruise to Jamaica and wished that I could get away to go with him. He offered to pay for everything, get my passport, and to take care of me if I could just get away. That wasn't happening at all! So, he went on his cruise and brought me back a bag full of little souvenirs from every spot he went to. We even had matching "Someone who loves you went to Jamaica" t- shirts he was just this dream come true guy to me.

I liked the way he held me close when he came in to kiss me with his big bubble lips. The way he took his time with me. The sneaking around we had to do just to make the little things happen meant a lot to me.

I can't imagine being a grown man interested in a girl that I was 13 years older than and sneaking around so her parents or siblings wouldn't catch us together. This day, I had to stay after school for student counsel to set up for the Sadie Hawkins dance. My teacher was super cool if we got the work done that needed to be done. I left my bag in her class and had to go back and get it. Since there was a phone in the classroom I used it to call Rome and he asked where I was, I told him school, he said, "Stay there I'm on my way." Mind you I'm with two of my girls waiting in front of school for their rides as well. I had been telling them about my boo for forever but they didn't believe I had it like that. About 15-20 minutes later as one of my friends left, he pulls up in a brand-new burgundy, shiny Dodge Charger, yes on rims, beat beyond Dre and limo tinted windows. She looked at me and said, "Girl, that's you?" I picked up my bag, put a fresh coat of Bath and Body Works menthol lip gloss on, said as a matter of fact, "Yup, that's him, see you tomorrow." We giggled and as he pulled up to the curb and got out to open the passenger door for me to get in beside him.

I was a little thrown too, just as much as my friend because for months I was so used to seeing the truck but I wouldn't let her know that. As we rode and talked I finally got around to asking what happened to the truck.

He replied, "It was time for something new, I love my truck but this is better, right?" As he leaned in for a kiss, I answered, "You right, congratulations." He said, "Thank you baby, you deserve to ride in the finest." Now in 2007 to 2008, Chargers and Magnums were the latest cars to be rolling in if it wasn't a foreign so I took it and rolled with it.

He promised to teach me how to drive and work all the buttons just in case I ever needed to use his car. As we were riding I noticed him making turns that did not lead in the direction of my house. He was just talking away so I interrupted him and asked, "Uuhmm, where are we going?" He replied, "to my house." Now, don't get me wrong, I wanted to go but I had already been late due to the fact that I had to stay after school, I was scared that I would be too late getting home with no story to cover. Moms was on to me, for a long time. I called and told her the bus was late I'd be home in an hour she said okay.

He parked in front of his house, got out to open my door, I was hesitant. He took both my hands saying, "If not today then another day, no rush baby Girl but I still want you to know where I live." That made me feel a little more comfortable but not enough so I asked, "What if another day is not soon enough for you?" Rome held me from behind and whispered, "then I'll wait" as we approached the door that opened to his studio part of the house. It was dark when we first entered but when he turned on the lights my eyes shot to the right side of the room that was filled with shoe boxes stacked close to the ceiling and racks of clothes. I was amazed. I never saw him in many of the shoes against the wall, let alone any of the clothes.

My parents had quite the tight leash on me so I didn't get out much unless it had something to do with family, The Tribe, or school. I remember having to climb up and sit on his high bed. I looked around, he had the basics. A television, movies, cool and clean little bathroom and I noticed a Cannon camera with three different lenses. He asked, "So, what you think? It's not much and neither is it forever but this is where I'm at right now." With a nod and a shoulder shrug I said, "Okay, its' not bad at all for now.
You're working towards something bigger and that's what matters." He said, "Why do you always know what to say and you so young? I like that shit man!" I replied, "I don't know but it's what I'm thinking so it doesn't get much better than that, that's just real."

He hopped on top of me pushing my back onto the bed as we began to kiss, his hands picking my whole body up to sit me on his lap and that's the first time I had ever felt my panties get wet. I was embarrassed to say the least but because we still had on our clothes I wasn't too worried until he reached down to touch me between my legs and I hopped up so quick and insisted that we go. He laughed and shook his head and followed me out the door. Rome dropped me off in our usual spot, in the back-parking lot of the suites, kissed me good bye and told me for the first time he loved me and had never met anyone so young that could make him feel the way I did. He made me promise that I would never leave him and no matter what we would be together and I did. But, little did I know that this was the first part of the game.

Mind control, where the mind goes the body follows.

So, as you can imagine things began to develop at a much faster rate and my young feelings began to get involved. Our conversations got a little deeper and longer every time we'd speak. I didn't own a cellular device at the time so we would set up a time for him to call the night before and I would sometimes turn the ringer off the phone so it wouldn't wake my parents. We were still living in the Budget Suites off Rancho and Lake Mead; the red light would flash on the phone when it was ringing and I knew to then answer it because it was my one and only. ROME.

HE SHARED HER

She wanted this night to be so special. She emptied her heart like an empty vessel. She didn't really know what she'd think after this night but she did put up a good fight with all her might. She told him she was ready but she couldn't stop shaking or seem to keep steady. He took her to his house with a thousand candles lit about. She jumped in the tub of roses and bubbles not knowing this satisfaction came in doubles. Got out the tub, hopped into a robe while he lit a light fragrance incent stick on the stove. He came in, rubbed her down with body oil. It felt good, so good that her love for him started to feel hot, her body felt as if it were a stove bringing a simmering pot to a boil. Turning her over and kissing her ALL OVER. It was at that moment she realized, she was just a tad bit drunk but still very much sober. It felt so good up until this point. Things started to get a little louder in that joint. It was over just a few hours later, the second and third time being much greater. After wiping all the moisture and sticky love stains from her skin, she went to retrieve her clothes and put them on but he stopped her. He helped her undress all over again and gave her large body towel, covering her beautiful yet youthful light skin tone, immature perky breast and freshly shaven vaginal area. As the door swung open, the body frame of two more young men made her feel doubt, fear and unfathomable terror. She quickly jumped to her feet and asked, "What the fuck is this shit, what ya'll think ya'll about to do?" The younger one who she knew was familiar replied, "Baby, we got you the homie said we good too. Let us be good to you. "She fought them off but by then it was too late. This night was all but great, nor exciting anymore. A few more hours had come and gone as if tomorrow never existed, all she could feel were her cold, frozen toes in her flip flops taking the long, shameful walk home. Her mind then allowed her emotions to roam, to absorb the pain that she'd now have to find a new home, for safe keeping and storage.

She thought this night would be great.

This was an experienced to be made, in just a second that moment was taken.

She realized it was a living nightmare and when it really happened all I could think is

I'VE BEEN SHARED.

BY: K. Nicole Howard (February 17th, 2004)

MY ROME'

I was at the finish line, my junior year of high school, had a solid nigga in my possession and I was getting things done, school and relationship wise. I was now going to his house regularly after school for "sexy sessions" is what he called them. He exposed me to a lot of things, one of them being what it was like to be with an older guy because I didn't consider him to be a man even though I was young. Sexually he would remind me of how I felt to him. From the inside out. How much he loved being my first and his intentions on being my last. Rome was the guy that fell in love with a young girl that loved him back but fell in love with the fact that he would be expose her. Expose her to the game, teach her the game as if she were his student. All so she could play it on him just as much as all the other niggas she was to encounter in the future. It was with him I learned how to orally please a man, the importance of swallowing and not spitting, how to pose for a home photo-shoot when I was with my man, how to be open or at least willing to learn something new. Sometimes, we just laid up but most times we didn't. By this time, Rome and I had been rocking for some months now as a couple, I would say roughly a year. There was a particular weekend I remember him speaking about. He asked me to plan to stay at P's house for the weekend because his homeboy was having a party he wanted to take me to. He gave me some cash to buy something nice to wear and gave instruction to wear something sexy and matching underneath.

As he asked, I made plans to babysit and bought something to wear during the week. I asked P if she would be joining me and she said, "Naw, I'm in, not feeling it tonight have a good time, be in by 3:30, latest 4:00a.m." I told her I would text and call as well as be sure that I was in the house, showered and ready for dance rehearsal we had at 1:00pm that next day. Once Rome got to the crib to pick me up in the white DENALI, he got out to open the door for me and had to stop dead in his tracks to take a few seconds to observe his P.Y.T. Yes, I was fly that night, for sure. I had purchased a blue denim Baby Phat bodysuit with gold buttons from the crotch up to the breast. I let the top three buttons stay open so one could get a peek-a-sneak at my perky breast that sat up just right in my *Frederick's of Hollywood* lace bra that came with a matching G-string that Rome would be eating me out of much later.

I've always had a voluptuous, proportionate body type, so basically baby was on the thick side. My matching gold Baby Phat four inch heels with gold accessories and small clutch threw the icing on the cake. Cold part is, I still had change left over from the $500.00 he had given me to purchase a dime sack of weed to roll up, throw P a little something for covering and put the rest in my cute little clutch I was carrying for the evening. When I got to him I hugged him tight and thanked him as always for making sure I was straight. As always, he smiled and shook his head and said, "Baby, it's really my pleasure, thank you for making it happen for Daddie." I grinned, "Daddie tonight? Okay, I hear you" I said sarcastically as he shut the door and we drove off. Our conversation was light as we drove and smoked his trees on the way. He explained it was his best friend's birthday party, there would be strippers, alcohol, drugs, all that I could ever need. He reminded me that I didn't have to partake in anything I didn't want to or feel comfortable with, which is what he would prefer, for both of our safety. Rome stayed strapped and had demonstrated more than just a few times that he would not hesitate behind what he thought to be his, which just so happened to be ME in most cases! He also spoke on the fact that he had been telling his boys about he and I. How much he cared for me, how excited he was for me to be finishing my last year of high school so we could be together the way we should be. In that moment, I felt my face turn up in the sourest way humanly possible. Like what grown ass man tells his friends, his girlfriend is barely legal, under both 18 and 21 years old, to top it off was still in high school, smart and fine as hell. I slowly adjusted my face before he noticed my disgust and discomfort in his statements about us.

So, when we arrived at the house it was a huge house off the new North side of town. Straight off Camino Al Norte right before Tropical Road, the houses on the left-hand side of the street. My initial thought was nice crib! It was a gorgeous house and had about 20-30 cars parked all the way up the block. My nerves all went to my stomach to entertain the butterflies that occupied that space. It must've been obvious because Rome reached over the middle console to grab my hand, he reassured me that I would be great, I was with him so WE would be good. In that very next breath he reminded me of how lucky he was to have me on his arm and how excited he was to be enjoying my company while flaunting me off to all his people.

I touched up my lip gloss quickly before Rome came to the passenger side door to assist me out. As we walked up the driveway people seemed to be staring at Rome but I soon noticed that they were staring at me once they had spoken to him already. This was nothing new to me at all, for some years' people would be caught staring at me as if they were stuck. As if I was someone famous or familiar when in all actuality, I was just me. It wasn't until years later I came to understand a little better why they were so intrigued with just little ole' me. I heard my grandmother Ozzie say once when I was a little girl,

"Souls recognize each other by vibrations not appearance."

Once we entered the home through these huge, white double doors there was an open floor plan there were two bars with a stripper on a stage between the two. At the very top of the stairs was a DJ, I would never forget it. Holding onto Rome's hand as his debonair shined bright in the dimly lit house. We walked through the vaulted ceiling home and I was introduced to some of the goons, the plug, and needless to say I felt the burning eyes of some of the trap spot rats trying their best to burn through my jumpsuit but my booty was too phat. To go from just thinking I was "THAT BITCH" to now irrefutably knowing "I AM THAT BITCH" was just enough to make me turn it up and smile back at it.

We finally made it to the backyard, where there was a domino game going on, women and men in a hot tub, another bar and bartender. Over to the right of all the action sat his best friend. Presumably the VIP section because that's where two broads sat to the left and right of him almost just as gorgeous as myself but missing the mark by visible degradation in their posture and physical appearance. Before we approached his best friend, Rome's voice echoed loudly across the entire backyard, "Happy Born Day P!" Hopping to his feet dropping marijuana crumbs out of the Backwood that occupied his hands, he greeted Rome with the warmest hug and most beautiful pearly white smile money could buy. Quickly he turned his attention from Rome to me. His deep light brown eyes caught mine and it felt as if I could feel his hands gliding down every curve of my body. "And you must be Nikki, nice to finally meet you Queen!

You know you got my man's nose wide open with yo' beautiful ass, right? Be good to him baby, cause you got it FASHO! Iight Rome, you were right, she's all that man, you did that playboy."

I seductively licked my menthol lip gloss, thanked him for his kind compliments and kissed my dude before excusing myself to go get our beverages. As I glided away, through the crowd, past the domino table I could feel all eyes on me. The looks on everyone's face was asking the same question, "Damn, who is she?" … one of the first of many memorable moments that evening. When I finally made it across the backyard, past the pool to the bar I ordered two Hennessey and Coke's, one with a cherry in it for myself to add a little feminine touch to a stiff drink. While I waited on the bartender to mix those for me I slightly leaned on the bar counter top and took in the view of beautiful people having such a grand time.

I couldn't help but mentally give myself a pat on the back for being able to even be in such an atmosphere and kill the scene at only 17 years-old. I looked over at my Rome as he smiled, pleasingly while his best friend talked his ear off. My mind awkwardly drifted back to the compliments his best friend paid me and the fact he called me a queen. That was the first but something about it felt good. Whatever it was would have to wait until later though because our beverages were ready and Rome was waiting anxiously to watch his baby work this room on her way back to his arm. After an hour or two of good vibes, drinks, and a compliment filled conversation I excused myself to go to the restroom as if I hadn't been about three times already. When I walked through the house the stripper was wiping down the pole as her voluptuous body gyrated to the sounds of Marquis Houston's *Naked* which happened to be a personal favorite of mine. When I made it to restroom I was trying to rush the urine out of my body, one because there were people at the door, two because I wanted to see what the dancer was going to do to my song. Before I could flush the toilet good enough and button my jumpsuit up Rome came busting in the door. "Nigga! What the fuck, can I pee in peace, I told you I was going to the restroom" I said frustrated because I was in a rush to see the stripper and get these people knocking off the door. He came in and locked the door, "You know this our joint. Come here girl!" He sat me on the corner of the sink, pulled my arms out of my jumpsuit and lowered it to my knees.

As I said before I knew what my nigga liked, he got a glimpse of the lace G-string and began to nibble away at my vagina through the lace panties before pulling them to the side and going to work. As the crowd continued to bang on the door all I could focus on was the water that leaking from my body as if a pipe had burst. When I gathered enough strength after what felt like forever I rubbed his braids, smiled at him before he kissed my lips to share the sweetest, and I assured him that we would finish this up later.

Satisfied with his services but annoyed that he had chosen to do this right when the stripper was going on, I wiped myself down with some warm water and paper towel before buttoning my jumpsuit, touching up my lip gloss once again and heading out the door. Once the door opened, Rome right on my tail, we both observed the looks on the faces of the occupants in line, chuckled and kept it pushing. As I was making my way back through the home, hand in hand with Rome I took just one small glimpse and was paralyzed, stopped dead in my tracks. There was a beautiful, 150 pound, Halle Berry look alike gracing the stage who was dancing to the most beautiful song I had ever heard, *Slowly* by Tank. She had a few tattoos on her butter cream soft skin, one which read LUCKY on the small part of her back. She had the whole damn house in the living room watching her every move, throwing money, everywhere, women and men. The expression on her face was pure sensuality, seduction at its best in my opinion. She seemed to get sexier as she sucked the energy and attention from the crowd of people gathered on every side of her. She then began to walk down the stairs that were off to the right side of the stage, behind the bar. When she made it around she grabbed a chair and Rome's best friend, it was over, she went to work. Hand stands, booty clapping, hip rolling and everything. The way this woman commanded the attention of every soul in the house and enticingly pleased this man for his birthday was something new and exciting for me. Although her occupation involved taking her clothes off for the sexual stimulation of others there was something about it that really threw me for a loop. I liked the money part of course because it seemed to have no end, it was raining, literally raining money on this woman. On the flip side, I questioned if the only thing Lucky must be proud of is her body? What about her mind, her creativity and her emotions, would they ultimately become something of little value and importance?

It is depressing to know that some women think that the only thing valuable about themselves is their body and what they can do with it. In that moment, I considered stripping as an option for myself, especially being that graduation was around the corner and I had big plans on moving out and away from my family for a while. That is what grown people do right? The show was over and Lucky was still the main attraction. Shortly after the crowd had dispersed, Rome and I spotted Lucky and his best friend ducked off in a small corner, headed up the stairs to his bedroom as he walked slowly behind her taking in all her glorious curves. I shook my head and smirked, saying to myself in my head, "Men are such vultures." Rome made his rounds letting everyone know the party would be over soon. He left his best friends' cousin with the responsibility of seeing everyone out safely and keeping all under control. As we made our way to the door Rome swirled me around for one last glance and whisper in my ear, "I see how you was looking at baby, she can be ours too if that's what you want." Giving him that look like, nigga nice try, that's a negative, knowing myself he could hardly handle my young ass on a good day. In a year I had become quite the force to be reckoned with when it came to our "sexy sessions".

We made our way to the truck, once in he leaned his seat back, as well as mine and insisted that we finish what we had started. While in the backseat, spread eagle, the passenger back door flew open, there stood his best friend in awe. Rome never stopped what we had going on to address his friend or even tell him to shut the door because it caused the car lights to come on, he just kept going in.

With my eyes, low-key locked on his friend I gave in and gave my first show until he tried to hop in the action, of course Rome wasn't having that. He pulled himself together and got out to chop it up with his boy. "DAMN KRISTIN! YOU GONE BE A BEAST." My last thoughts as I beat the sun with a couple hours to spare.

BLACK SHEEP

Blessed with a curse.

Not ever knowing for sure.

Only because the gut feeling is missing.

No decision made.

Knowingly and Pure.

Loving the solitude.

I, ME, and MINE.

So many siblings,

Yet it's so hard to change my vocabulary.

How God did the apple fall so far from the tree?

Black Sheep.

By: K. Nicole Howard (July 15th, 2012)

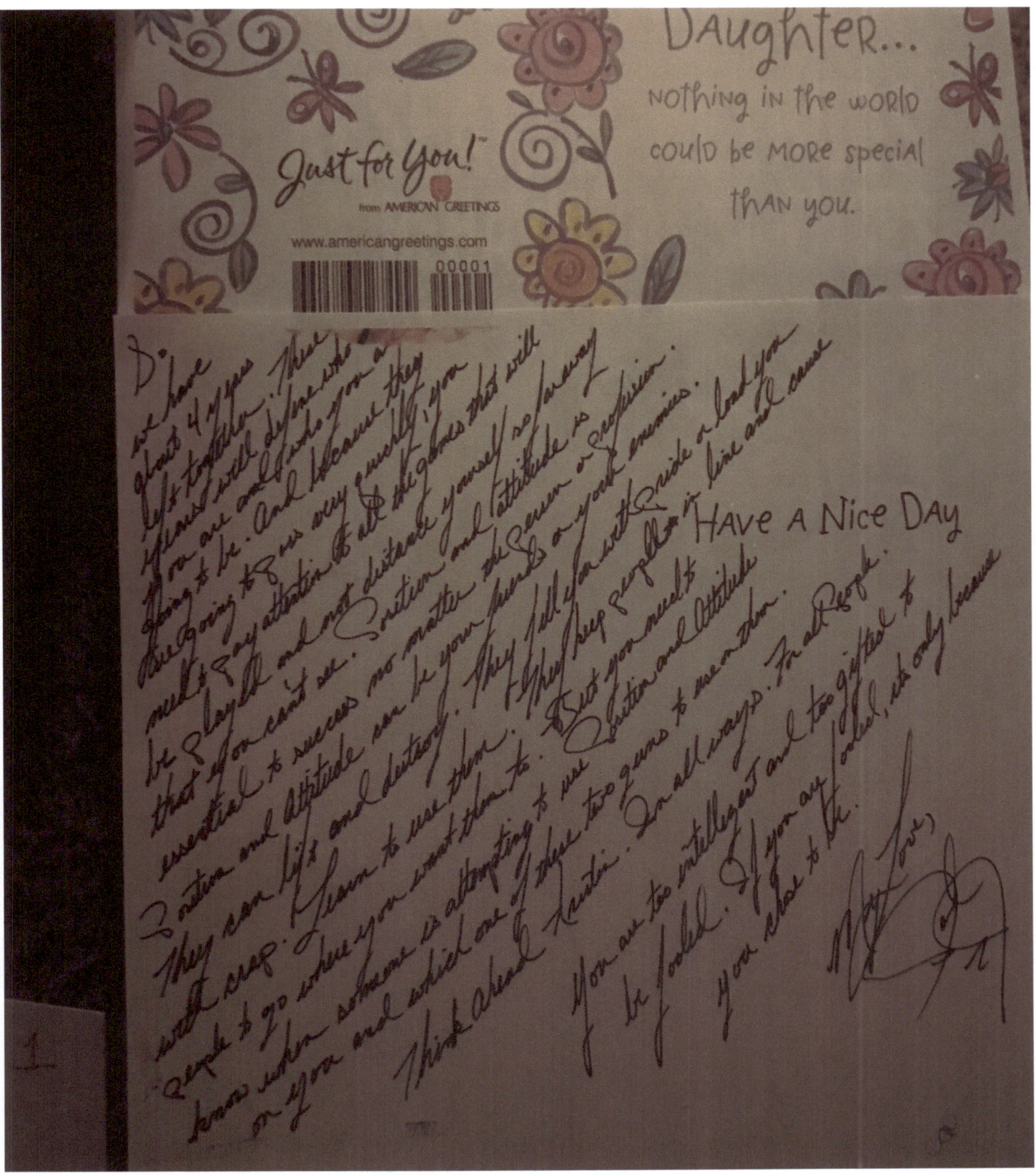

Daughter...
nothing in the world could be more special than you.

Just for You!
from AMERICAN GREETINGS
www.americangreetings.com

D,
we have about 4 of you. Let's get together. These 4 items will define one who you are and who you are going to be. And because they are going to pay very carefully if you neglect to pay attention to all the gloves that will be played and not distrade yourself so far away that if you can't see. Sometimes and attitudes is essential to success no matter the scene or suspicion. Sometimes and attitudes can be your friends or your enemies. They can lift and destroy. They fill you with pride or load you with crap. Learn to use them. They keep people in line and cause people to go where you want them to. But you need to know when someone is attempting to use sometimes and attitudes on you and which one of these two guns to use on them. Think ahead Kristi. In all ways. For all People.

You are too intelligent and too gifted to be fooled. If you are fooled, it's only because you chose to be.

Have A Nice Day

Love,

LIFE ON THE OTHER SIDE OF THE DIPLOMA

High school graduation for me had come and gone, I was now 18 years old and had only two things on my mind, GET MONEY AND MOVE OUT. By this time, I had my first job working in a group home setting with individuals who had mental, physical and intellectual disabilities. To have just graduated from high school it wasn't bad money at all, but when you're single without a child, those taxes hit you hard every pay period. After researching and moving around a bit, I decided to get into the adult entertainment business. I knew just the right person to contact who could help me look in the right direction, my favorite cousin Rosie. Single mother, doing her thing as well and always had it popping. I had stolen a few of my first cigarettes, Benson and Hedges premium menthol from her. I would've been caught had she been counting. She was the real PLUG! She knew some of everybody, everywhere, doing some of everything. At the time, we really started to kick it I was initially just the baby sitter. I could have a friend over if I liked but no parties, no strangers, and she had to approve before she left. She also had a friend who had come from California to stay with her until he got on his feet. Rosie was a heavy weight in this strip club called *The Palomino*. It was the male revue that she and her clique of friends ran with and had established some great relationships with as well. Every male dancer had a different themed show with props included. Best male revue I had ever experienced. I tagged along a few times and even got the opportunity to work the door for one of the all-white party events.

The friend that lived with her wanted to start a big black booty strip club because there weren't any at the time in Las Vegas, anywhere. I spoke with my cousin about jumping into the adult entertainment business. She was my cousin but I always had a closer relationship with her because she kept it real with me, no matter the cost, sparing no feelings what so ever. She always said, "Cousin you're beautiful. You got a little hood in you with a whole lot of GOD, don't lose that Baby Girl." Rosie never judged me, put me in harm's way and most importantly she always respected the fact that we were family but I was grown and whatever decision I made she would be there to support me and rock anyone's cranium who dared to try her or her little cousin. So, once *Urban Night* started popping upstairs in *The Palomino* club I looked to her for guidance and a little exposure to the ends and outs of this part of the game.

Make no mistake, Rosie was it, still could be if that's what she desired. I attended a few shows and had the privilege of hanging out at some of the events and club parties that were going on frequently for advertisement purposes. Not too long after I was auditioning for Mr. Foreplay upstairs. He kindly told me to continue to come around but at that time, I wasn't ready. He needed more from me and he knew I could give it, I had it in me but the timing wasn't right. I took his advice, practiced in every mirror I encountered and on every guy I called myself entertaining. I was relentless and persistent with this dancer thing, for now it was back to the drawing board.

I was still living with my parents, siblings and Kaila's cat Chloe' in the Budget Suites. I had a few new associates at my group home job but I only had been rocking with two on a consistent basis. One a homosexual male named Brent and my Hispanic best friend Jackie. They were my two best friends other than my girl Deez I met in high school. After kicking it with Jackie, she later introduced me to my best friend Breezy. I expressed to Jackie and Brent how bad I needed to get out from around my parents and out of the tight living situation I was in. Jackie said that she was looking to move out soon and so was Brent.

One night, not too long after this conversation things got heated between me and my parents. I packed the only way I knew how to, in bags! After packing all my trash bags with all the clothing items, I felt a sudden sadness come over me as Jackie helped me put all my bags in the trunk of her 2000 Mercedes Benz. She hugged me as I cried in disbelief, fear, guilt, and remorse. She reassured me we would be fine and we could stay at her house with her mother and grandmother until we got up on our feet. We stayed there for about six months before signing the lease to our own apartment. It was Jackie, Brent and I. We had a three-bedroom townhome in a nice gated community on the North side of town. I was so happy but still felt some kind of way because I had not been in contact with my parents or siblings all that much. Things were going well for the three of us until Jackie lost her job at the group home first. She had brought with her most of the living room furniture and a few wall decorations. Brent and I were trying to be nice about the situation and not jump down her throat constantly. We were sure that she knew rent would be due soon so we spoke briefly a couple times and left it at that. She agreed that she would have it because all our names were on the lease, she wouldn't do us like that.

Exactly two weeks before the first of the month I get a call from Brent while at work, telling me that Jackie's room and the living room had been cleared out when he arrived home from work.

I remember being at work, first off in disbelief, secondly steaming hot, lastly blowing Jackie phone up to no avail of course. After this you can believe I vowed to never get myself in another roommate situation.

Soon after her departure my eldest brother, Kenny came to stay with me. His timing couldn't have been a better, I needed some family within close vicinity and I had a brand-new niece Keyonna Nicole, my namesake whom I loved to spend all my time with. For the remaining 6-months of the leasing agreement this set up was perfect until Brent and Kenny lost their jobs. Brent found another quickly, still with just the two of us it wasn't enough to cover groceries, utilities, travel expenses, and rent. We ended up having to break the lease and I moved to my aunt's house. At the time, she had plenty of space and I could still function and move around like I needed to. While at my aunt's house I was introduced to my greatest 1 TIMOTHY 6:10.

(FOR THE LOVE OF MONEY IS A ROOT OF ALL SORTS OF EVIL, AND SOME BY LONGING FOR IT HAVE WANDERED AWAY FROM THE FAITH AND PIERCED THEMSELVES WITH MANY GRIEF'S). -- NEW AMERICAN STANDARD

SIN'S WAY

You said you wanted to know her,

Well, her she is.

Outside of working, hoeing and all the other bizz,

Here I am, sharing with you what I love the most.

We've both opened up a little more over time,

Me, myself?

I think that deserves a toast.

You've shown loyalty, friendship, genuine care and give me intimacy like none other,

Waiting for the day I'm introduced to your grandmother as your all, everything, friend but most of all your eternal lover.

You seem to love hard,

When you give, you dig way down deep,

Thinking of your sickness I cry every night, releasing my sorrows from my heart as you sleep,

I weep.

I pray and plead with God that he never, not ever need you more than I,

And takes you away from me.

In July '09, I had no idea who I was really setting myself up to meet,

But, looking at you I see the kind hearted, angels' reflection that lives inside of me.

Seconds, minutes, hours, days, weeks and months have all gone by,

The material things are disposable and you know my heart is pure when I say,

"Yeah, that's my dude, #1 guy." HE'S ENOUGH. No extras. No sides.

With Sin J., there's never a dull moment,

All business man, no franchise.

Every day he lives it, loves it, and owns it,

His swag is different only because of the high-profile haters that feed his ego,

Seriousness of Sean Carter, fashionable to be Sean Combs.

This is Sin's Way, if you ain't know,

Now, you know.

By: K. Nicole Howard (September 4, 2009)

MEETING SIN

For a while I had known about the personals section, as well as the escort section on Craigslist.com. I would get on there and search for odd jobs, for men or women looking for companions, dinner dates, or escorting businesses that were hiring. It was simple, you got to the category in which you are interested in, browse the ads and reply with photos and your contact information. This day I came across an ad that was right up my alley. The ad was for young women ages 18-25 years old who wanted to model or had prior modeling experience, willing to travel, create moments, and live life to the fullest all while making thousands of dollars a day. After sending over some of my best bathroom pictures and some my friends had taken, I quickly got in contact with the author of the ad, whose name was Monah (MOAN-A).

Monah worked for a guy named Sin. To my knowledge and from what I was told he was the one I wanted to know. He also had the final say so in the hiring process. I set up a date and time to meet with her and Sin for a photo-shoot in Summerlin for the very next weekend. I just knew I had hit the jackpot. I drove my aunt's car to a nice complex of condominiums, I called Monah and let her know I had arrived. I parked my car, said a prayer and walked up the stairs confident.

Once inside I looked around and admired the cleanliness of the place and the spacious layout. Monah was kind enough to give me a tour of the three bedroom condo and explained she was his secretary. She also explained that Sin conducted meetings, mostly business from this location when he was in town. She was responsible for the up-keeping of this location while he was away, which was frequently. She also went on to tell me how kind my eyes were, how pretty my smile was, she admired the gap in between my two front teeth and perfect body. Per Monah I was exactly what the doctor ordered and some. She explained that they were in the adult entertainment business, as she put in the ad. The first step in the process was to confirm my identity and age, from there I would be meeting with Sin so he could get a feel for my personality, some job and criminal history. As far as the adult entertainment industry this would be my first real job so I wasn't worried about anything besides being everything physically that the job required and Mr. Sin being just as thrown by my natural beauty as Monah had been.

While I waited, I was given something to drink and handed the house phone to speak with Mr. Sin briefly about him being over an hour late. I have always been respectful about other people's time so I expected nothing less. After taking the phone and saying hello, I heard the sexiest, baritone voice say, "Please, my apologies for my tardiness, it's been a busy day but Monah says you're beautiful so I can't wait to finally meet you. I'm sure your pictures don't do you any justice," he said. I smiled and replied, "Who knows but I'm here." before hanging up the phone call. As I walked to the backroom where the office was, I looked on the walls for any sign of a woman, family, or children. I couldn't find one, not one, not even a photo of this Mr. Sin. I finally made my way to Monah as she sat at the desktop going through visible emails that contained photos of numerous women, "Did you speak with him? Cool guy huh? I apologize but I'm sure he'll find a way to make it up to you, that's just the type of guy he is.", she said. "Yes, I spoke with him, thank you. I'm not sure about him being the cool guy but he's definitely, without a doubt a very late guy.", she laughed. I felt the need to ask some questions out of curiosity and to pass the time, "How long have you known Mr. Sin? What is it exactly that I will be doing? How much traveling will I be doing? Will I be going alone? With Mr. Sin? Will there be other chicks going? You? Or what?" She shook her head and giggled a bit, "Well, first I applaud you on asking questions, your mother and father should be very proud of you, they didn't raise no fool. I've known Sin for some years now, he's a great man, and we met some years ago, in California. He doesn't trust many, if any when it comes to his business so that says a little bit about my character and loyalty to our friendship. As far as what he has planned for you, I'm not sure. More than likely you will be traveling with him in the beginning. He travels frequently back and forth to California, so plan on keeping a bag on standby. When he's ready to go, he's ready to go, stay ready so you never have to get ready Baby Girl. Did I cover everything?" Skeptically, I nodded as I heard the heavy feet running up the stairs, not too long after the keys dangling in the door, at that moment I felt a sudden nervousness come over me.

"Monah!" He screamed down the condo halls while making his way to the kitchen to grab a Squirt soda pop from the icebox. "In the office", she replied. I was sitting on a bar stool next to her computer chair as I heard him come down the hall. I turned to look behind me and was breathless.

Smooth dark skin, about 5-foot 8-inches, 150-165 pounds' light, the deepest waves I had ever seen in a fade that were natural and hadn't come out of a box. He was a very tailored, wearing Sean John from head to toe, manicured, clean finger nails, YES! "Wow! You're gorgeous! Hi, I'm Sin, I finally made it, thank you for waiting." In my head, I'm thinking, "Nigga waited! I'd wait all over again if you asked me to" but instead I was very lady like and replied, "You're very welcome, thank you for the hospitality, your place is lovely." Not too long after the initial introduction we ended up back in the living room sitting and talking. He seemed to be genuine as well as fine. Fine as hell. He was a little on the shorter and thinner side which was not really my type but for him I'd make the exception. So, after conversing we exchanged numbers and remained in contact so we could do the photo shoot before heading out of town and introducing me to another young lady that I'd be learning from, she was a veteran in the business.

 He walked me down to my car on his way to his, it was a 2007 black Mercedes Benz CL 500 Coupe. We hugged and parted ways. I must have smiled the whole way home before my phone buzzed with a text that read, "You wifey and don't even know it yet."

Smiling even harder, thinking to myself *mission accomplished.*

UNTITLED

God took my cookies,

And gave me a cake.

When he was making you,

He made no mistakes.

Whatever guys gave,

That's what I used to take.

That habit I had to break,

You stayed and didn't walk away.

Which is great,

When you fucked up and went astray,

You sat and listened to every word I had to say.

Now, that we've found one another,

There will never be another for us,

No sister or brother.

Me plus you have become,

Fitting each other tighter than any glove,

One in a game called,

Puppy Love!

By: K. Nicole Howard (April 1st, 2004)

IT'S COMPLICATED

It wasn't long before we started hanging out regularly. He would pick me up from my aunt's house we would do lunch, late dinners sometimes. Sin lived in his vehicle and on his damn cell phone. He stayed on the go which was rare. Usually, by now I would've been to a man's home already but nope, not him. Sin spoke very highly of his daughter, cat, cousins, and loved his grandmother like nothing I had ever seen or heard of. When he spoke of his grandmother, I could see him smile from his heart which spoke volumes because I was a very family oriented person. He said, "One day soon you'll have to roll with me to L.A., that's where it's at man. I'll take you to meet the number one lady in my life." It was then that I knew we were on our way to being more than just friends and he cared for me. Sin invested in all the things money couldn't buy and I loved that most about him.

It had been about a month or so before we ever gotten around to the photo shoot, thank GOD. When we spoke on the pictures and their context it shook me a little but I also knew he was more than capable of making me feel comfortable. We were going for the exotic look that I had apparently covered already, naturally. Clothing would be at the bare minimum if any at all from what he said, very little make up and at least four different outfits. You can believe I was more than ready when that day came.

Sin picked me up, per usual from my aunts' pad around 4:00 PM on a Sunday. I was off from work and had gotten some rest. My best friend Breezy hooked me up with a job where she worked as a night auditor for a hotel called the St. Tropez near the strip. Sin and I arrived at the condo where we first met. Once out of the car I said, "Sin? How long is this going to take, I'm super nervous so don't laugh. This is my first time." He laughed, "Come on babe, you act like we about to rob a bank or something. We good, I got'chu, TRUST ME!" He leaned in for a kiss and I leaned back, rolled my eyes and made my way up the stairs to his office condo. I walked in expecting Monah but to my surprise we were alone, I sat my bag down and went to the icebox to get a bottled water for myself and Sin. "Hold on really quick. Babe! Come here, please", he said from the office room. "Yes, Mr. Sin?", as I walked down the hall. "Bring your stuff in here, we doing the pictures here.

Let me finish up this call, BE READY.", he said kissing me before heading out the door. I replied with an okay, whatever look because I had been around him long enough to know, those phone calls that required him to leave weren't short conversations.

While naked in a G-string and bath towel, trying to figure out what to put on first I suddenly remembered I'd told Breezy I'd text or call to let her know I was straight once I got there. She replied right back saying, "Okay girl, GET IT, I LOVE YOU! Hit me when you done, tell Sin hey." I told her everything, we were tight. More like sisters than best friends. I heard the front door open and quickly dropped the phone on the bed as if I had been caught going through his phone but before I could put anything on Sin was behind me running his soft hands up the back of my bare thigh, kissing every inch of skin in sight. "I don't know what to wear baby," I said. "Don't trip, you're good. We only need a few to start right now then we'll get you some professionally done. Deal? Damn, you so fine. Mmmmm!" he said. He asked if I needed anything before we started, I said no. After that, the rest was history. We had to have taken 20-40 different shots, they were all beautiful to me. He brought out something in me I had no idea I had. The ability to be sexy without any conscious effort, the shots of me looking away, smiling eyes but no real facial expression, he made me so happy even naked just as I knew he would. We laid in bed going through the pictures, laughing and enjoying one another space. It was dark outside by the time I had went to the restroom and returned to the bedroom to put my clothes on. Sin was on his phone again, sitting in front of the computer.

When he heard, me return he swung around in the computer desk chair and motioned for me to come sit on his lap, I made my way and took a seat. On the screen were all the pictures he had taken, I took the mouse and scrolled through them all. I had to pat myself on the back because despite the nervousness and being a rookie I killed it. For the photo-shoot to be in house and not professionally done, baby was damn near flawless. The last photos were coming up and I felt my irritation growing while he entertained his phone conversation more than what we had going on. I removed his hand from my thigh and went to get up but his grip on me was firm. He ended the call almost immediately, planted his phone on the computer desk and ran both his hands underneath my towel until it opened exposing both my breast and the thin, sheer purple panties.

I tried to act as if I was too upset with him to oblige, gently fought the kisses, listening to my own "No's" turn into long, soft moans until I couldn't deny him anymore. I felt my body give in completely because I didn't' have to say anything with my mouth. While he kissed me with his eyes he asked, "Would you say yes?" Drawing his body down completely on top of mine I let him feel my answer to all he had questioned. It was then our souls intertwined and whispered to each other, "MINE."

We had been to California two or three times in a matter of months, I had met his home girl Tasha who was a high paid escort in the business. The three of us had been to California together and that didn't amount to much once I caught onto what this really was. Tasha continued to do her thing while most of my time was spent with Sin, she didn't like that too much but it was whatever with me as far as any other broad went. Don't get me wrong, she was absolutely a gorgeous black woman and was very goal driven. Tasha's bread winner spirit is what I loved most about her. Once she was out of her feelings we vibed well together. I soaked up as much free game as I could while in her presence every time. Aside from her the only other game connoisseur I knew was my best friend Breezy. It wasn't long before I began to apply my own techniques to what I was learning from these two young ladies in my life.

Sin and I had been going strong for about 9-10 months before moving in together. Yes, finally I was out of my aunts' home. I had been in an accident with my girl Jackie and gotten around $3000.00 - $4000.00 from my settlement. After making sure to take care of my aunt and grandmother, I thanked her and shook that spot. Sin and I lived in Summerlin in a two- bedroom condominium off Cheyenne and the 95 Highway. I was working at an open top tour bus company on the Las Vegas Strip, which didn't pay very much but he was picking up the bill and making sure I was straight. Not too long after that I started to notice a change in his patterns. He wasn't coming home, well at least not home to me. He started to send my calls to voicemail, becoming upset because I wasn't making the money he would've liked me to make. I began to get fed up with him coming through just to get my half of the rent and him giving "hush dick". He gave me just enough attention to keep me from nagging him.

He never pressed the issue with me about becoming an escort though. I had already had a few blue and white-collar jobs and male friends on the side who assisted me in the stacking of my bread. All I was waiting on was for Mr. Sin to get caught slipping, he didn't make me wait long…he never disappoints.

Late afternoon, after being gone for two days with Breezy and Deez I returned to our home from work only to find my front door open with a key left in the door knob. I kicked the door in and called for Sin, no response.

As I walked through the apartment I seen our photos ripped to shreds, television knocked over on the floor, my jewelry box and jewelry scattered everywhere along with all the clothes and shoes that had been torn from the double-sided walk in closet. The mattress and box spring had been flipped off the frame and across the other side of the room. I was beyond furious. My first call was Sin, I would not stop texting or calling until he answered to this crap he had obviously brought not only to me but to our home where I laid my head. When he answered, I went for his jugular, "Really Sin? You don't even live here. I come home to my door kicked in, my things broken and torn to pieces. I would have never done anything like this. What if I would've been here when she decided to break in and go ape- shit crazy? I would probably be calling you from a jail cell nigga! You're fulla' shit, I'M DONE! Tell that bitch she can have your Sean Combs look-a-like, box perm wearing ass.", I said before hanging up the phone to lose myself in my tears before calling my best friends to come back, I needed them to comfort me. I knew there was another chick somewhere named Nicole because I had gone through his phone weeks prior to the incident but little did I know this place was in her name and she got the extra key from the front office. Nicole and I weren't the only ones but I was the one put in harm's way and that hurt me to my core the most. I packed the things I wanted to take with me and luckily my stash of cash was still underneath the carpet in the spare room and in the cereal box in the kitchen. I left everything as it was and added to the damage that had already been done before leaving and never looking back. Sin called and reaching out to me many times to no avail. As far as I was concerned, he was the past, I had no reason to answer, I knew in my heart he had nothing new to say. CASE CLOSED.

REDEMPTION

It's okay that you felt absent, and petrified, and insecure.

It's okay that you were drowning in self-hatred.

It's okay that you let your confident lay scorched, and your dreams charred.

It's okay that you let blackness invade your heart, and it's that you are still ashamed.

It's okay that you let the forged happiness over run the complexity of your tears.

It's okay that you forgot family, and in forgetting family, you forgot yourself.

Poetry calls to me every day,

when I'm sleep, awake, at work and at play.

If I only could find a moment

to travel these halls,

A poem is waiting to be set free

to be released from within these walls.

A poem of **REDEMPTION** for us all.

By: K. Nicole Howard (May 8th, 2011)

NO NEW FRIENDS.

Though things caved with Sin and I, staying gone from my parents' home was my biggest motivation and where I found a lot of my strength, in making my own way. I played every nigga I came across to my advantage and had some of the hardest conversations about my life. I had to take a step back and think about where I was headed if I didn't stop the smoking, drinking, and partying. By this time, I had auditioned again for Urban Night and made the cut. Major accomplishment for me then because I was so secure with myself. There was a commercial that would be coming on Spike TV, I knew my father watched that channel sometimes. There were also flyers being rotated around the city with my Mom's Tuna Fish and Dad's Baby Girl on them in a G-string. I couldn't stomach the thought of my parents finding out something like this from anywhere else but myself. One day before the airing of the commercial I spoke with both my parents about what I was doing and tried my best to prepare them mentally for what they might see. The night it aired, they saw the commercial.

I was nervous, excited, and motivated more than ever to make this *Urban Night* experience work in my favor. I had been around Mr. Foreplay for some years and watched his hard work and dedication manifest. He was still a male dancer himself but he was "THE BOSS MAN", meaning he didn't have to but he was humble enough to continue because he had bigger dreams. His dreams were bigger than just the strip club, fast life for him. I found myself admiring him and having gone to see a movie with him once or twice. I loved to pick this man's brain. Needless to say, he was the BOSS and I had a serious thing for a BOSS NIGGA! In later conversations, I found out that he didn't drink alcoholic beverages, smoke or get involved with any of his employees. His dream was to have other businesses, one being a coffee shop. He was so amazing to me but I had to admire him from a far. I still hadn't had any children, so no bullet wombs nor tiger marks. I was still killing it at 18 years old. I had linked back up with Jackie and Breezy on a money tip. We remained close, at least tried to anyway. Jackie eventually dropped off and did her own thing, which was cool because we ended up linking back up and working at *Urban Nights* together. For the most part, it was just Breezy, Deez, and myself. Long days, longer nights, sleepless days, nicotine filled nights. Most of those I spent with my best friend Deez, she had her own whip, own place, cool chick since were the girl's high school literature class together.

2009/01/02 02:06

We had been rocking for years, she was the ride and I was the supply. I was the "BAIT" friend from what many say. It made me no difference. I loved all my girls because we all brought something different to one another's lives. We were all so raw, real, and unique but most importantly, we looked out for one another like family. We functioned regularly, ran the streets, learned the game together and built a system of trust in one another like nothing I had ever experienced in life before. While dancing at *Urban Night* on Thursdays and working for a tour bus company on the strip I was killing, not to mention I had a cool little bench. My bench consisted of at least two D-Boys and one or two "Square Bears" that loved the mess out some Nikki.

I had an uncle who worked for Wal-Mart and wanted me to apply for the cashier position in the Pharmacy. First, my uncle didn't like the fact that I was a stripper. Secondly, he knew that by starting off as a pharmacy cashier after 9 months they offer you an opportunity to go to school, all expenses paid to become a pharmacy technician. I decided to continue to strip but take him up on his offer because I heard that a lay-off was going to be happening soon at the job I currently held with the tour bus company. It took me about a year to get myself together again and ready to move out. After receiving the job at Wal-Mart I was doing okay for myself. I moved to a one bedroom apartment, had my own car without a driver's license. Not to mention, I lived one block away from Deez and only two blocks away from Breezy! Perfect CHAOS!

Both Deez and Breezy had significant others but that never slowed us down. I was the single friend with "ALL-THE-SHIT". Our days usually consist of purchasing an eighth of some fire trees, wine, Four Locos or any alcohol we had enough money to piece up together and buy. Breezy and I were the ones that always had the plug on the trees and Deez had the whip. If we had gas money and could smoke her out we knew we were good. We also got heavy with popping Xany bars (Xanax). It's also known as Alprazolam, used to treat anxiety and panic disorders. It works by enhancing the effects of a certain natural chemicals in the body. When you mix it with the alcohol, man, crazy things happen.

Deez had been spending time with her guy, who was from "The View", along with listening to Young Jeezy "aka" The Snowman with me and put me onto the Blue Dolphin pills.

This is one of many different types of Ecstasy (MDMA) pills, commonly a round blue pill with a stamped dolphin. Yes, to only be 18-years young, soon going on 19 we were heavy weights. Going super hard or going home, it was the only way!

The car I had was a gift from one of my guy friends I worked with named Chris. He was cool, Caucasian, older, and a virgin! Chris had to be at least 38 or 39 years old and was saving himself for marriage. That was all good with me because he wasn't the type I planned on giving any of my pretty kitty to. We became great friends, he some paid bills and didn't mind helping me one bit. In return he wanted time and genuine friendship. Chris and I would hang out after work or on off days together and I began to see how genuine he was. I didn't mind his corniness or loud laugh that reminded me of Goofy from the Mickey- Mouse Clubhouse. He was sweet and cared about my well-being. You can almost bet that all our co-workers were in his ear at work about me just playing him for his money and taking his kindness for weakness. It was because of those same co-workers and their interest in my life that Chris and I fell out bad and he took the car back to the car lot and never spoke to me again.

While having the car, I had accumulated many tickets for driving without a driver's license and even a jay walking ticket, just ridiculous! I couldn't make court and risk missing work so this meant failure to appear and having warrants put out for my arrests. I had gone to jail a couple times and made a conscious effort to pay my fines, do my community service and stay far away from the jail house. I was not the jail type of chick, not to mention every time the police ever caught up to me I wasn't even the person behind the wheel and I had just gotten a fresh full- set and effortless slay from my hairdresser Mya.

Prime example, I had gotten home from working a 10-hour shift at Wal-Mart, took a shower, rolled up and started the $5 bin series of documentaries on serial killers that I've always loved to research. The ones like, Jim Jones and Charles Manson. My phone rings. It's Breezy, "Girl, what'chu doing? You off? What's up with tonight, you trying to get out, call Deez and see if she'll swoop you? Ya'll come over here, I got some bars and drank at the house. Just bring some trees." she said. After a short conversation about family, niggas, and other stuff I said, "Iight, I got some trees, let me call Deez, I'll hit you and let you know what's up."

Before getting off the phone she had to remind me how serious she was about being around her girls, she was going through quite a bit with having a baby boy, crazy baby-daddy, family and a new dude. Plus, everyone knew Nicole will say "iight" but after my body hit my warm, chocolate brown satin sheets and I hit the weed, it was over, lights out until I wake at midnight looking for the party.

Deez was just getting off at 9pm that evening and said she would be over to get me by 10pm, so I knew to have the "bleezy" rolled up and set for rotation by the time she got there because I would have to hear about her Mom, nigga, and work problems next. It didn't take her long at all this time to get here, so I was left to assume she didn't have any trees of her own to smoke or needed to get out bad as well. I threw on my favorite grey *Juicy Couture* sweat suit and we headed out the door. Deez was really my best friend, she always trusted me.

Most of the time she let me use her car even though she knew I didn't have a license or drove me to the money because seldom times we weren't on anything else. She had been with me to numerous bachelor and private parties, I trusted her with my life and my money. That was rare for me, not to mention all the trouble we had been in together from high school up until now.

We arrived at Breezy's about 15- minutes later, she had gotten a new spot and this was our first time visiting her. She was right off the US-95 Freeway and Martin Luther King. Deez and I parked and were walking looking for the apartment before we heard the blasting sounds of Lil' Boosie's song, *Cartoon* come from the right of us, the downstairs apartment, we knew then we were in the right place. Breezy came to the door after we knocked twice, "It took ya'll bitches long enough, finally get to see the pad," she said. Her place was fully furnished, ducked off and nice on the inside, though the neighborhood wasn't the best. It was a surprisingly spacious, two-bedroom and two-bathroom apartment. It was just enough for her and her little family she was starting. I made myself right at home after inquiring about the Xany bars she promised and she came right out with a whole bottle, a fresh filled prescription. I popped 2 of my three pills requested and relaxed. We popped our bars, sipped, smoked, laughed, listened to music and chilled with some of her people before we ran out of drank and Swisher Sweets.

Breezy and I agreed to roll with Deez to the gas station around the corner on Bonanza and Martin Luther King to re-up on everything. We got ready to leave and I had the keys in my purse so initially I was driving. "Girl, you sure you straight to drive? Nicole? Give me the keys, I'll drive." I remember Breezy and Deez saying. "Are ya'll serious right now? That's how ya'll gone do me, I'm good. Get in the car, please." I said. They didn't argue with me anymore about it, we all strapped up and headed to the gas station.

While sitting at the light on Bonanza a Metro police cruiser had gotten behind us. I made the turn into the gas station and parked at a gas pump before he suddenly decided to turn the red and blues on us. I turned the car off and remember bits and pieces of that whole situation. What I do remember was not being able to walk in a straight line, I couldn't hold a conversation with the officer nor did I have on any shoes for some odd reason and of course no valid Nevada driver's license. This night in 2010, I was taken to Las Vegas City Jail to be booked on a DUI charge. I don't remember any of the intake process but I'm quite sure it was the same as all the other times I had been to jail. Once changed into my orange jump suit and giving all my complimentary personal care items I remember making it all the way up the stairs to my assigned bunk and falling all the way back down the stairs. There were officers all around me but their faces were blurry. The next time I woke up, the sunlight was piercing my eyes through a small, rectangular window, surrounded by dingy off white bricks for a wall.

I was sore as all out doors. There were so many bruises on my body and I couldn't even begin to tell you how they got there. There was an older lady in the same cell with me, once she seen me sit up in the lower bunk bed across from hers she immediately asked was I okay and how I felt. The cell door was open and in came 2 other chicks that looked to be near my age telling me that they thought I died because I had rolled completely down the stairs before hitting the concrete floor hard. All I could do was laugh because my body was too sore to so anything else. I asked them as many questions as I could about my situation and it felt good to know it really wasn't the worst. I had been booked on driving under the influence and would be release that evening with all the other inmates getting out. In jail terms, I had been "O.R.ed", basically they would be taking me at my word that I would come back to court instead of charging a monetary bond.

I called my parents first to let them know I was okay and would be home, to my apartment that evening sometime. I called my girls, Breezy and Deez of course to let them know I would be at the pad, I also would be needing a re-cap of all the events that led up to this horrible experience. I would also be needing the trees to be rolled up, wine ready and a hot bath. They didn't fail me but the story was hilarious and embarrassing all at the same time. Nonetheless, I was just happy to be back to the gates, mi casa!

UNEXPECTED

If things went the way I'd expected, I'd be living a fairy tale by this time. But, because this is reality as usual things began well and so suddenly had unwind. These months of adulthood have by far been such a struggle. If this thing isn't pushing, dealing with this person is a juggle. I've graduated high school, which happens to be one of God's many blessings to me. I've moved out from underneath my parents' wings. I've worked, paid bills, partied and a whole lot more. From this party to that one. I've even conducted my own different kind of party behind closed doors. My hair, nails and feet were and are always whipped to the "T". Not for only me but so other people can see. It is okay to live life to the fullest, be single and free. On top of my "square" 9-to-5, I danced for various occasions. The men gave money for the simple entertainment I gave somehow this was amazing.

Quickly I found myself falling away from my teaching much deeper than ever before. I'd lost my job, not because of my doing but because it was bullshit from the beginning. If you continue to read, you just might learn and catch my ending. Prescriptions and weed began to take me to a place I loved to get away to. I had a feeling other than pain but when it was over I felt I needed it to cover up the feeling. I thought the people I loved and cherished could see the residue as I if I were completely bare, nude. Looking on Craigslist.com for adult gigs that would help me out in one way or another. One finally came through. I found myself in some strange man's motel room. Compensation was $100.00, pressing him for information on whether he worked blue or white collar.

Here I sit with nothing, alone. My pretty little light skin is now pale, no longer have 10 but 9 nails, my body resisting food, my voice no longer has a sexy and soft tone, the style of my hair is wearing off from two-weeks ago, and I'm almost completely gone. All I have now is everything that God's given and has not taken away. My 18-year-old life, my talent to share in my writings and all my five senses. Everything deducted not even reduced. The message…

Expect the *UNEXPECTED.*

By: K. Nicole Howard (December 27,2008)

"E" MPTY PURSE

I was still working at Wal-Mart and stripping at *Urban Night* upstairs in *The Palomino* strip club in North Las Vegas. Everything was going well considering the fact I was frequently going on weed and alcohol binges. I had been to court for my DUI several times just for my public defender to keep postponing my court dates and trying to find other evidence that the policeman that stopped me didn't read me my rights, which by law is a must before they take you into custody. I still loved living alone. As always, I had a select few come through, pay a bill or two, spend a night, burn something and make me smile bright. Shopping sprees were just something light. I was not to be played with. All the guys in my life knew that I'd cut you off and have your replacement meeting you at the door on your way out. NO FINANCE, NO ROMANCE. I had bills to pay just like everyone else, I also enjoyed being the boss, running my own show. So, as far as I was concerned you could get with it or get lost.

That all changed one Thursday night while on my way home from work. I borrowed Deezs' grey 1995 Honda Civic to go to the club because I no longer had a car of my own and couldn't run the risk of the police stopping me, taking me to jail for the tickets I had failed to pay and show up to court for. I was meeting one of my guy friends at this spot-on Las Vegas Boulevard called *O.G.'s*, it was another strip club. He had been telling me to check it out because he knew once I got in I could kill it. The only thing in that spot was dope head broads and older white chicks who had regulars, basically sugar daddies. While driving down Las Vegas Boulevard, one hand on the steering wheel and the other digging through my GUCCI tote bag for my lighter I had to swerve out the way of an apparent drunk driving. "FUCKING DRUNK CUNT", I said. Hot, steam coming from both my ears because my GUCCI tote bag and all its entirety had fell over onto the floor of the passenger seat. Thankfully I had reached my destination and was able to turn right into the packed-out parking lot next to a 2009 silver Lincoln Navigator with limo tint on the windows. That drunk broad was the least of my concerns in that moment, I was now out of the Honda Civic in pursuit to regain the contents of my tote bag and on my cellular device letting a nigga have it for thinking it was okay for him to question me about my schedule and where-abouts.

He had a whole ass family at home that included a wife he claimed to be unhappily married to who had just given birth to their third child only four months ago. We'd been an item for about a year now but his inquiries were not only out of line but came at the worst time ever. I had almost been in an accident with a drunk driver and in the process of dodging that bullet my bag decided the passenger seat floor was a better fit than the passenger's seat. After hanging up the irrelevant phone call with no warning, I finished picking up the last of all my things from the floor of the car with my lighter being the last thing in my hand. As I closed the passenger's door on the car and made my way back to the driver's side. Before I could sit down there was a brown skinned, six-foot something man saying, "Excuse me, excuse me miss?" I ignored him as much as distance would allow. He was moving swiftly and before I knew it he was just on the other side of the driver side door, which happened to be the only thing separating us. "Look, I'm really not in the mood for anything you may think you want to say to me right now. So, no you can't know my name and I don't have a number." I said rudely but super serious. He laughed but continued, "I just saw you on the phone so I know you have a number but are you okay? I see that car almost hit you and by the look on your face right now that's not the only thing that has you out of your element", he said. His observations seemed to be on point so I sat my bag in the seat, along with my phone neglecting to respond to Mr. Unhappily Married Man's text message.

Once I was free of all other distractions, I could get a good eye full of the hazelnut King that stood in front of me. At best, I would say he was 6'1, about 180-200 pounds, had the most beautiful even toned espresso brown skin, a smooth and silky goatee to match the waves in the fresh bald fade he wore. Whomever his barber was needed to be booked on murder charges because the line up on that thing was to die for. He was dressed in a black and white USA *Polo Ralph Lauren* short-sleeved collared shirt paired with *True Religion* jeans and *Air Jordan Retro* IV's (fours). He extended his soft, veined hand, "My name is Forever, nice to meet you beautiful, since you haven't given a name yet. What you got going, its almost 5 a.m. and breakfast is next for me. If you don't have any plans, gracing me with your presence would make my night, my day actually."

I couldn't with this gentleman for some reason, his style was different, his whole approach seemed to be a little rehearsed but refreshing. Not to mention his style was impeccable, his Lincoln Navigator was just as clean as he was.

"I go by Nicole but whatever you'd like is fine by me. Beautiful fits rather well and feels good too." I said with the sweetest smile, semi-smirk on my face. For some strange reason men always fell for the mystery that was in the chortle I had. It gave that "it's something different about this one" vibe, I knew it and used it to my advantage frequently as a one up! We shook the strip club parking lot not much longer after I had given him a name and a number just in case either of us had gotten lost on the way to the *IHOP* we agreed to meet at. Once we made it to the restaurant and got seated I didn't really have much of an appetite so I ordered fruit before Forever ordered his breakfast. He had been the first African American man I'd ever met that ordered his steak medium well and eggs cooked over easy. While we waited, the conversation exchanged between us was quite interesting and strangely fulfilling. I felt like we had been friends or had at least been acquaintances. We had more in common than what I thought we'd have, that seemed to balance out our differences quite well. He was from Milwaukee, divorced, one son, prior military, and lived right down the street from me. "I shop at your job, that Walmart all the time. I've never seen you or I would've been at you, you would've been mine a long time ago," Forever said. I replied, "Yeah, ok. I hear you." As the sun began to rise we both found ourselves yawning and drained to say the least but not wanting to leave one another's presence.

Forever invited me back to his apartment where I slept for about an hour or two before leaving. As I slid off the left side of his bed I searched the top of the dresser for a pen and piece of paper. On it I wrote, "Thank you for breakfast, had to go, just in case you forget it's in your phone as Nicole#2." Thank goodness he lived in the apartment complex right next to my bestie Deez because I was lit'! I parked, showered and hopped into the bed right next to my best friend smiling. For once I felt like I might have run into the man of my dreams.

Forever seemed intelligent, one child which was rare and had this "best of both worlds" type of swag to him. I knew he was into the fast life I just didn't know to what extent but that would come with time as he becomes comfortable with me, I'm sure.

I was feeling him but the feeling was different this time around I could see myself being with him, being whatever, it was he needed me to be. He had a few friends and ex-military buddies that lived here in Las Vegas but no family. Before I closed my eyes to go to sleep I had already convinced myself that I would let him have me, I needed him around me, I had to be his family.

FLAWED

The **BEST**.

By far better than the rest.

The **TRUTH.**

You know the root.

The **RIGHT**.

I can accept wrong at any time.

I am…

The **IMPERFECT**.

By: K. Nicole Howard (August 11th, 2010)

FIRST OF THREE

It's been said that we only fall in love with three people in our lifetime. Yet, it's also believed that we need each of these loves for a different reason. Often times our first is when we're young, in high school even. It's the idealistic love—the one that seems most like the fairytales we read as children. Now, I've never been one to believe in what others say or what I may read but this one kind of love stuck with me now that Forever and I were living together after only 3-4 months of talking. It was my idea that he moved into my apartment one because he was always at my house anyway and two because he had a roommate situation going on at his place. There was really no need for him to be paying bills at both places, it was cost effective and convenient for both of us. Things couldn't have been any better for us. My family loved Forever. My parents loved him, siblings, it went all the down to my grandmother. He continued hustling of course and went to school using his G.I. Bill from the military. Of course, there were days that we could live without; arguments that should've never happened and days I threw all his clothing items over the balcony of our second-floor apartment, but what's life without a little excitement.

What I loved about Forever was that he loved me from a place of growth. He understood that I was only 19 years-old, going on 20 year old soon and so he let me breath. It was with him that I did most of my experimenting with sex and drugs. Some days, when I was off of work we'd stay in, do lines of cocaine, chain smoke *Newport* cigarettes and have the wildest most satisfying sex ever. It was euphoric and exotic to me what my body was capable of consuming this many narcotics… literally and figuratively speaking.

My juices were never ending and his erections were everlasting.

It was our haven, our judgment free zone but he also knew that I only did these things with and for him and him alone. I still kicked it with my girls Deez and Breezy when my time would permitted between being wifey and working. I got a chance to meet a lot of his close friends and family that lived-in town or came into town to visit. I had been around REAL pimpin', heavy weight D-boys, as well as some of his married military friends. It was cool.

They always said we were going to be married one day and I believed them. Hell, I believed him when he used to tell me. I was still working at Walmart and doing well without having to go back to stripping. Yes, Forever only put up with me stripping for about a month into our relationship before telling me to drop that whole situation. For him, it was worth it.

He couldn't stomach it. Our bond was so strong that he went with me and always brought at least one of his guys along just in case something popped off. He stayed strapped and his boys remained ready for anything, always. After about a year into our relationship, we had been through so much. He went to jail a few times, linked up with some snitches and caught his first case and experienced money issues. Not only with him, but while all of this was happening to him, the police had finally caught up to me for my many failures to appear in court. Things were legitimately bad for a few months, but we stayed together through it all. The most devastating thing was just right around the corner and had been for 8 weeks, we just didn't know it yet.

Yup, I was pregnant! Forever was ecstatic and would talk to my belly. He made sure I never over worked, he cooked and was an amazing provider. He already had one son whom we kept in contact with and would go see regularly from his prior marriage. So, for him this was what he wanted and with me, the woman he wanted to be with for the rest of his life, let him tell it. Me on the other hand, I wasn't ready. Financially, I didn't want to bring a baby into a situation where we weren't stable. Neither was I mentally prepared to be a mother, I understood the sacrifice I would have to make as far as my life no longer being my own but that didn't mean I was ready to make it. I wasn't fond of being a "baby mama" either. That was the ugliest thing to me… ever. I wanted to be a wife and have a family. Wifey and wife ain't the same thing. That's all I had ever wanted for myself and having the same set-up for my child was non-negotiable.

For days on in I had battled with the idea of aborting my child or keeping it. I even told my parents who weren't necessarily thrilled but they understood my position and gave sound advice on the pros and cons of either play in which I ultimately would have decide to make. After much deliberation, I decided that Forever and I would be parents in 7 months and would soon be married after.

It had only been three days after coming to this place of mental peace that all of our dreams were shattered. I was being rushed from work in my mother's car to Mountain View Hospital because I had gone into labor.

Once in my room in the hospital, after the testing and doctors' fidgeting all around me, I was awake, exhausted, and in an indescribable amount of pain. I was very appreciative to have been surrounded by so much love. My mother, father, grandmother, aunt, and of course Forever were all at my bed side. I didn't remember much after going into the hospital. I do remember however being told that I had a miscarriage due to me having an Ectopic pregnancy. An ectopic pregnancy is when the fertilized egg attaches someplace other than the uterine wall, most often in the fallopian tube. (Therefore, it is sometimes is called a tubal pregnancy.) In rare cases, the egg implants in an ovary, the cervix, or the belly.

In my case, the fertilized egg had attached itself in my fallopian tubes which was the cause of my severe abdominal pain and lack of menstrual cycle. I was down for almost 3 weeks after being released from the hospital. Forever and my family were my rock. I decided that I needed to move back home for a while and get myself together. I needed to start fresh. On top of it all, I needed the financial support. I could no longer afford to take care of all my bills, court fees, and day to day expenses. Forever and I weren't in a good place for a while after but he came with me when I moved back home for just a little while before we decided to part ways. We were still together just separated and getting our lives in order. We both needed space and time to recover from all that we had gone through. Not only that but we needed time to heal from what we put one another through in the process. Three months later I was pregnant again and didn't think twice about getting rid of it. A month before my 20th birthday, I had my first abortion which was just as painful, if not more for the simple fact I willingly threw my baby in the trash at just 5 weeks of gestation. Now, back to the dirty grind because I said this being back home situation would only last a short time.

Forever and I loved one another very much. He was my first for many things. He was the first life I had ever had the pleasure of caring, sharing, and experienced love with in every kind of way. I was working at a tour bus company on the Las Vegas Strip when Forever called me saying, "Hey baby! What's up? I miss you, I LOVE YOU SO MUCH KRISTIN.

You already know I'm locked up and I'm going to be down for a minute but I want you to keep in touch with me. Never turn your back on me baby. When I get out we gone live the way I promised we would. You won't have to work and if you want we can try for our baby again. My time short so write me or make sure I can call. I love you Wifey." That was the last time I had spoken to him in about a month. Once he got out we linked up. I knew he had the plug on the Xany bars and was purchasing for a friend but I popped three in the process. Old habits die hard, that's what the old folks say. I spent the night with him at one of his friends' houses not far from mine. He made love to me like when we first met, promised to marry me after his time was over and the rest is a blur. When I came home I can somewhat remember hearing my mother's voice in a panic and my father carrying me up the stairs of the house. I had no under garments on, basketball shorts, and my mother said I reeked of sweat and sex. It felt as if I had slept for days.

When I woke, my mother was at my bed side with both bottles of pills I had purchased asking me what was I thinking and what was I going to do because I couldn't continue this path. I could see every ounce of hurt in her face and felt every tear that streamed in slow motion down the cheeks of her beautiful hazelnut skin. I couldn't answer her right then. Everything was still in slow motion… I was zombie from the Xanax. My cell phone kept blasting so I finally reached over the opposite side of the bed to answer it and it was Deez on the other end telling me to log into my Facebook. Someone had leaked a naked photo of me claiming I was a home wrecker and to be aware. I didn't entertain it much because I couldn't process everything way I needed to. I hung up the phone and cried hysterically! I cried until I had fallen back to sleep. The next day the picture was gone. From what I'm told to this day, the picture was very tasteful, Deez and Breezy held me down. They defended me to no end and went to war with everyone, including the very upset woman whose dude had been obviously cheating on her. They also made sure the photo was deleted and never again was the situation brought back to life.

As far as Forever and I, we hadn't spoken in years before I had come back to Vegas pregnant with my son in 2013. When we crossed paths, it was easy getting back on speaking terms. He let me know how many nights he dreamed about me being by his side now that all was on the up-and-up since his release from jail.

How he missed his rider, how young but solid and A-1 I always was with him. No more strange faces, no more open cases. He also told me about all the watching he did from social media, which would've meant a lot more to me if I would've known then what I know now. We remained friends on Facebook throughout the years, made time to see one another despite relationships and a few new significant others we may have had down throughout the years. We still have so much love and respect for one another and sometimes I still have the desire in me to want to be his **FAMILY**. Again. For always. Forever.

CORRUPTOR

Cold as the blood from the fangs of a vampire.

Fresher than the Louie and Prada in Kanye's attire.

Talking internal suspicion?

She can make a pig's partner wear a wire.

Sleeps by day, grustle (grind and hustle) by night.

Never yawning, half ass-ing, or tired

Consider the eyes of her at the right or wrong moment,

10 minutes later.

She'll ask, you'll give your soul as if you never owned it.

Beauty and sophistication like none other.

If she's deadly, lethal is the nickname of her birth mother.

At losing, she's never been all that great.

She let me preview a millionaire's real happiness,

Giving her the combo to all the safes.

Her inspirations,

You'll find them to be very odd,

Something like Johnny Depp in *Sweeney Todd*.

Griselda, Meech, Jigga, Ricky and Halle are just a few on the list,

The ones behind the scenes who still reap the benefit of leading actor/actress

Engage in all the glamour and glitz.

This young lady in the crowd, you couldn't point her out.

Just give me one opportunity to occupy some of your time,

Because paradise isn't a location but it is a state of mind.

By: K. Nicole Howard (August 26th, 2010)

ONLINE SHENANIGANS

The year was 2010, I was doing very well for myself. Still, I was going hard in both my social and work life. I had kept my job at the tour bus company, where I worked with my twin brother Kyle and my bonus brother Steven. He was my brothers' best friend whom we had practically grown up together with. My life was quite simple; work, family, friends and church from time to time. I was still smoking weed and cigarettes. I had given up the pills, unless I was going out on a special occasion. Even then, my pill of choice was an ecstasy pill, preferably a Blue Dolphin or Triple Stack. I was still living at home with my parents until I could figure out my next move. I really didn't have a desire to live in Las Vegas anymore. It was truly a gamble. Las Vegas had given and taken much from me. Even the weather was a gamble.

I had a few choice guys I would date and chill with from time to time. It wasn't long before I was over them as well if not instantly. None of them seemed to have any long term, let alone any short-term goals for their lives. Between baby mama drama, not really being a challenge or bringing anything different to my table, I got bored. I was experimenting with the online dating scene quite a bit and decided that I really liked it. I could be whomever it was that I thought I wanted to be. I could limit how many people I wanted to know, meet with or simply us to just pass the time. I was blessed with the gift of gab anyway and being able to be in control of the whole situation from the comfort of my bed was amazing. I was using sites like *Plenty of Fish*, *Mocospace*, *Craigslist* (personals section), and *Tagged* was my favorite out of all of them. *Myspace, Black Planet*, and *Black People Meet* was old to me so I didn't even bother with those. I had quickly been put up on game though as far as the people who used these sites, everyone was looking for or in need of something. Most men were jail/prison inmates, fresh out looking for a come up or pimping. Most of the women were hoes. They were made up of desperate, overweight, attention whores looking for a sugar daddy. It was because of that, I didn't bother limiting myself to just men. I was open to having a beautiful lady friend as well. After having a girlfriend for a short lived few months, I learned that women are extremely clever and better at playing silly little games. It was also with my girlfriend that I found out that when you're a mother you cannot neglect your children to have the life you didn't get to have. The girl I dated had three children, two-teenage girls and a toddler son.

They were always around the adults and being exposed to things that they shouldn't have been. It was then that I placed both my parents on a pedestal and vowed to always honor and care for them because my siblings and I were never exposed to the dangers of life because of my parents doing. They were great. No drinking, smoking, twerking, parties, or men/women in and out of their bedroom. Just Mom and Dad, I was so appreciative to have that, now I see it was something rare.

After my girlfriend and I parted ways, I began talking with this guy who lived in San Diego, CA. on *Tagged* whose name was Mr. T Montana. He seemed down to earth, not too pushy and he didn't live far. I didn't really care for "Cali niggas" though. I was 21 years-old had my fair share of Californians and I discovered I didn't like the West Coast men. I wanted to experience something from down South, East Coast or Mid-West, plus I was still hell bent on leaving Las Vegas.

I kept in contact with Mr. Montana, we messaged and talked over the phone frequently. I liked his swag, from what I could see online and in some of the photos he had taken and sent to me. He was 6'0 exactly, braids that hit his shoulders with 4-5 beads on the bottom sometimes, his dress was clean and crisp the way I liked. He had these beautiful Chinese looking eyes with long lashes that looked as if he had bought them and had the individually attached. Mr. Montana had the pretty white smile to match everything else as well. We kept things online and over the phone for almost four months. He let me know he had business in Las Vegas as well as some friends and family he wanted to start visiting. He had mentioned coming to town to see them but not neglecting to slide me while there as well. "Now that I know you, I have that much more of a reason, and a little sense of urgency really. You're beautiful and single. So, I just want to get in your face and see if that's really the case Lil'Mama." he said during one of our phone calls while I was on my lunch break.

He was cute but I still was a "Bad Bitch" and had no intentions on taking this nigga any kind of serious. In my mind, this is Las Vegas, Nevada where anything with anybody at any time could happen. I had the privilege of not having to see they ass ever again in life if I didn't want to and I was perfectly fine with that. So, with a little concern, I was cool with whatever he wanted to do because I had no intentions on taking this "Cali nigga" any kind of serious, as I said before.

New Years was approaching and I kept seeing this DJ that worked at dozens of clubs and always loved having me in the booth next to him. He was DJ'ing at a club in Town Square called *The Blue Martini*, I had never been but agreed to tag along. I had proven to him on numerous occasions I had an awesome ear for good music so he valued my input when he was working. He wasn't all that cute and was partially deaf in one of his ears so he spoke kind of funny. Having a chick like me treat him like he was all that mattered and someone nobody could say they had been with or ever seen before, yeah, he was killing it. Major ego booster, props and pussy came rolling in for him I'm sure, but he always treated me like a lady. He never failed to continuously make sure I was taken care of whenever we were together. I was already out for New Year's 2011 with my girls. When I finished up with them and their shenanigans I linked up with my DJ buddy.

The date was January 1st, 2011, I was 21 years-old and loving every bit of being able to go where I wanted, when I wanted with no issue. I was already out and about and decided I'd drive myself to the *Blue Martini* where my buddy was DJ'ing. I loved the atmosphere from the jump. It was as sophisticated as a place could get. Something about it was phenomenal. The DJ booth was small but I had a front row seat to all the action, including the dance floor. For it to be New Years the club wasn't really that poppin' to me so I got on my phone to see what everyone was up to. When I looked at my screen I had six unchecked messages in my inbox on *Tagged*. I scrolled through them to find that 2 of the messages were from Mr. Montana. He said was in town on some business and for the course of the holiday and wanted to check me out. So, after messaging back and forth for a while I agreed to let him come check me out. After giving him the address to the club, it didn't take him but a cool 15-20 minutes to make it my way.

Before he arrived, I slid to the lady's room to freshen up a bit. I had mad love and respect for my DJ friend so, I stepped in front of the Blue Martini to meet Mr. Montana. He was dressed in *LEVI* 501 jeans and a cold button up shirt, braids fresh as usual with no beads this time, smelling like *Jean Paul* cologne, I knew that scent all day long as it happened to be my oldest brother Kenny's favorite. He didn't disappoint and I guess I didn't either from the way he held me tight for a few seconds after our initial greeting hug.

He said, "Damn! This is crazy, I can't believe it's really you. Your pictures cool but you live in person lil'mama. You super right." I blushed, then said, "Thank you. The feeling is mutual." He asked did they have a restroom inside he could use so I walked him in the direction of the desired destination. On our way, he asked, "You pop pills? I got one for you if you want." I really didn't know him and from the look I had given him he already knew what was up. "I already popped but I'll pop one with you so you can see it's all good." He gave me mine and swallowed his before disappearing to the restroom. I had my drink in one hand and the pill in another. After a brief examination of I said, "Fuck it."

When he returned, I let him know I was in attendance with the DJ, who was a good friend of mine but I'd call him once I left. He smacked his lips in disbelief but agreed to wait and answer that phone call. I stayed maybe an hour after that and left to go home. The whole time I was there I was in contact with Mr. Montana but soon after 5:00 AM I decided to turn it in. I was barely beating the sun home. By the time I made it to the house, I'd given Montana my address via text so I wouldn't be driving drunk. I showered and changed into my Chicago Bulls sweat suit, glanced at the clock it was 6:00 A.M. We were winging it and I had never actually met anyone online before so I didn't want to go too far away from home. We ended up getting a room at the Cannery Hotel and Casino on Craig Road. Mr. Montana had everything covered once we made it to the check-in desk. I offered to put it on my card but he refused it saying, "Maybe next time, this time is on me, I gotchu'. You feeling that pill yet," he asked. I replied, "Yes, but I'm more awake than horny if that's what you're asking." He laughed, I already knew what was up. We made it to the room where we began a great conversation about the things I had done and experienced, what I wanted for myself in the next 5 years and what I was willing to do to get there. I explained to him that I had always been a free-spirited young lady. That I'd try anything once, I mean how else was I supposed to know whether I liked it or not. How do you give sound advice or a review of something you've never experienced? That was my philosophy about life in general. I couldn't stand a broad saying giving your man oral is gross if she never even had a penis on her lips, let alone her mouth, or down her throat.

The sun was beaming into the window, I couldn't take it so I got up to shut the shades. That pill had kicked all the way in because I had cotton mouth something crazy and was sweating profusely. I asked if it was okay to shed some of the clothes I had on without making him uncomfortable. I got rid of everything except my G-string, socks and weave. I could tell he wasn't ready when he spotted my two nipple rings. I hopped in the shower to rid of the perspiration that the pill had me feeling like was running from every inch of my body. I returned to a fully clothed Mr. Montana again! I had made up my mind that I was not leaving this room without getting mine. I graced the bed with my naked body and began to do it for myself as he watched. I took his hands and put him to work immediately thinking that would help his limp, lifeless penis. Nope! No action, nothing was happening there and he wasn't even embarrassed. The way my natural vaginal juices were effortlessly flowing, all I could do was giggle in between moans and shake my head as to say, "Nigga, you suck for this, Cali Niggas."

"Don't be laughing, I popped two pills. This usually doesn't happen to me, especially off a pill. I gotchu next time for sure. Don't even trip." Montana said. My body language didn't lie and I've never had a good poker face. I had all I needed and was going to get from Mr. Montana, quite frankly I was disappointed. To be honest more so for him to even think there would be a next time was hilarious to me. I gathered my belongings and began to dress, letting him know I had a modeling audition and work later that day so this New Year's "rondevu" was over. I hope he enjoyed himself because giving him anymore of my time was not in my plans. All Mr. Montana would be getting or should expect from me here on out is a **HARD TIME with a side of COLD SHOULDER!**

HARD NIGHTS

I remember long drives before we ever began to take flights.

Accepting 40's and 50's. I need all mine is what I'm about,

Believing your every word,

In you I had no doubt.

Missing holidays, birthdays, family and friends,

Determined to keep my promise to trap it out with you to the very end.

State-to-state, city-to-city some trips alone, most of the time you were with me.

Sometimes hit and missing but you had a star,

Most times I recall, we were winning.

Watching my body go from super thick to extra lean,

Catching you laid up with a bitch while for you WIFEY was trafficking.

Motel to hotel, room to a suite, bucket to foreign,

I fed you, your momma, your kids and me,

All in hand never to save one piece.

Drugs to stay up, drugs to fuck before I lay down,

I know what loyalty is,

A bitch who still is and will always stay down.

Hard Nights.

By: K. Nicole Howard (February 26th, 2014)

SECOND OF THREE

If I was following the "three loves in a lifetime theory", Montana would be my second love. The second love is supposed to be your hard love—the one that teaches lessons about who we are and how we often want or need to be loved. This is the kind of love that hurts, whether through lies, pain or manipulation. I thought I was making different choices from my first love Forever, but in reality, I still made the same choices out of the need to learn lessons—but I hung onto Mr. Montana much longer than my relationship with Forever. Early on in mine and Mr. Montana's relationship there were signs I seen that I knew would be unhealthy, unbalanced and narcissistic. There were an abundance of emotional, mental and even physical abuse, manipulation and high levels of drama. Sadly, this is what kept me so addicted to our storyline. It was the emotional rollercoaster of extreme highs and lows and like a junkie trying to get a fix, we stuck through the lows with the expectation of getting back to the high. With the kind of love that Mr. Montana and I had we kept trying to make it work. When trying to make it work became more important than it actually working you have to think whether it should actually work. It was the love that I rather we wished was right.

Mr. Montana and I dated long distance for about 9 months, he lived in San Diego and I was still in Las Vegas. I went to visit him once or twice and he came to Las Vegas regularly for business. Of course, when he came, he did so baring gifts every time. From being with him all the time while he was in Vegas, my suspicions about him being a big-time drug distributor became a reality. He was making plenty of moves in my town. Not to mention it was a big plus for me because I never had to purchase weed or pills after meeting him. I was always straight when it came to supporting my bad habits. We had talked about him moving here but we decided that I would go, and experience California first then move back here if I didn't like it there. It wasn't long after moving to Southeast San Diego, California that I found out things weren't as he made them seem. Even still I was in love with this man and more than willing to make it work. Montana had not long been out of prison from doing a two-year bid. He was still on paperwork and wasn't supposed to even be leaving the state of California when we met New Year's or all the many times he had come to visit the first 9 months of our relationship. In my head, he put himself at risk of a violation for me, I owed him my loyalty.

I was determined to be that solid chick he needed, that he deserved and solid not by liquid form. I wasn't working for about 3 months before I went back to what I knew to be true to me, yup *Craigslist*. I let him know that I didn't want to just sit at home and watch him work endlessly alone. I began to get regular tricks through the site but later was put up on game by his cousins' girlfriend about what was really going on and what was expected of me. She had been hoeing for 2 years with his cousin and Montana was looking for the same, a stomp down, bottom bitch. Knowing this, I found the nearest library and began to research the adult entertainment business "aka" prostitution business. Yes, I was a self-taught hoe. Two of the first books I read where, <u>The 48 Laws of The Game: PIMPOLOGY</u> by Pimpin' Ken with Karen Hunter and <u>Pimps, Pastors, Pulpits and Prostitutes: The naked truth</u> by Bishop Woodrow H. Dawkins Jr. Along with the books came music. I noticed my choice of musical motivation had shifted from Fred Hammond and Sade to Messy Marv, Pimp C, and Sugga Free. Not that their music wasn't good and they weren't talented. It was the message. The reassurance I needed to know that this is what men liked and needed to have in their life. This is the bitch I must be to survive in this relationship or even be semi-appreciated.

There were many fights and arguments due to my unwillingness to totally jump right into being his hoe. I was super hard headed and didn't agree with selling my vagina and giving all my money to a nigga who couldn't keep it real from the jump about what he really wanted. I was kept in the house other than when I was out with him and his friends. It was only one time I went out with some of the girls he had introduced me to without him and my God was that the wrong thing to do. Montana had attitude for days and was very short with me because I wanted to do my thing just as he was.

The infidelity was of course another obstacle. We were in his town and he was addicted to searching the dating sites for other prospects. Desperate, Montana even turned my *Craigslist* search into a way to meet with other girls to smoke, drink and chill. He would have me around chicks he knew he fucked and swear up and down he didn't. The embarrassment I felt was the worst feeling I had ever felt. Montana always was a very talented lyricist. He was a beast when it came to making music, which was another reason to believe in him.

The things he did with words was beyond amazing. Had our money been right, in my head we could shake this garage studio and really blow up doing this thing.

My dreams for us began to flourish. My dreams were just that, dreams. He had other plans and it wasn't long before I found out he wasn't thinking that far ahead for his life so, how could I? Montana had two daughters whom he loved very much but of course the baby mama was the real headache. I instantly fell in love with the girls after meeting them. While he was out hustling, I would be home with them, cooking, cleaning and tending to all my wifely duties. We were living in a room mating situation with his cousin and his cousin's girlfriend because of the financial situation we were in with just his income. Weed, alcohol and pill popping became my usual go to in order to refrain from thinking about my reality. I was still in touch with Forever who was in a relationship but told me on many occasions if I needed him to hop a flight he would. He was also willing to drop whatever relationship he was in to be with his wife, ME! I was still determined to be that chick, the same ones I had read about in the *Nikki Turner* and *Zane* books. Blinded by lust, money, the misconception of love and loyalty. I had mentally made up in my mind that I had to give this thing a real shot for it to work. I had already done a lot of things I said I would never do, this was small to a giant.

Some of our first trips we took were in California of course because I was a rookie and going any further than that would put his freedom at risk. California was also known for its pimping and hoeing culture anyway, what better place to start. I started playing the internet in Santa Barbara, CA. I loved it there. It was like a small town with beautiful neighborhoods. We blended in well as the happy couple we were while the money was coming in. It wasn't long after that I was exposed to some of the worst tracks in California. Tracks are hoe strolls, you walk the streets in hopes that a trick would pull over and request sexual favors in exchange for donations (monetary gain). When the internet was slow or dry in the day time I would walk tracks like El Cajon Boulevard (San Diego), International Boulevard (Oakland, California) and Sepulveda Blvd (Los Angeles, California).Though the going rate for services were $40-$250/per service, I was all money in. I had been robbed with a knife by a trick I wouldn't even acknowledge because he was riding a bike. He took my satchel and my phone.

Montana was in the car with his other pimp homeboy, at a gas station up the rode but I kept him on the phone so he could always hear what was going on and I reported ever street I was on or crossing so I would never get too far. The night this happened to me I was terrified, he came to me not even two minutes later and chased the guy down until he dropped his bike and hit a fence on Montana. "You okay baby? You been seeing him ride all night, you want to go back to the room or you good?", he asked full of concern but still wanting to not miss any money because I had been killing it since 6:30 P.M., it was now midnight, the internet would be popping soon. I still had all my money because I knew better than to keep it in my satchel, therefore it was always in between my cheeks, in my shoe or in my hair that I kept tied back into a ponytail.

When we returned to the motel room I couldn't catch my breath nor could I stop my tears from flowing. Montana was livid but once I stopped to take in what he was cursing about, it was about me not doing what he said, I went too far, I didn't tell him that there was a guy on a bike riding back and forth. I could not believe it, I was hurting, I had been robbed, a knife put to my throat and he was upset with me. I refused to go back out and played the internet, just *Backpage* and *Arrows*, which upset him even more to the point I was being called all kinds of "squares" and "faggots". From me, not one fuck given! If Montana needed the money that badly, he could go out there and get it.

⭐ **~-**$3XxY ~ $ituation**-~**

Hello Beautiful Ladies! Let me start by hoping you've had a productive and prosperous day thus far! Now...lol......

Some may say, a woman like me is hard to come by...but I assure you am the real McCoy! A hopeless romantic looking for that special someone that I can shower with love and affection and quality time.Not I, am not looking for someone who is already established. I'm looking for someone where we as a team can build and expand. I'm a real woman who strongly believes TEAM WORK MAKES THE DREAM WORK;TOGETHER EACH ACHIEVES MORE....I'm willing to roll my sleeves up and help you build, willing to get into dirty the trenches and start a solid firm foundation. Looking to inspire,motivate and uplift you and push you closer to your dreams. If you're looking for someone who knows what they want out of life,determined in achieving her goals,then am the person for you.About myself, am 22 years of age college educated . My zodiac sign is Cancer .I'm completely single,that hasn't been married. I do not have any kids,however if you do it isn't a problem;I adore and love children. As far as characteristics, am nice down to earth,honest,caring,I have a funny sense of humor,loyal,open minded. Mixed descent. Lighter complexion. I stand at 5'5 I weight 130 pounds,I'm thick far from fat or sloppy I work out.I have long eye lashes,almond shape light brown eyes,full kissable soft lips. So,if this interest you and your serious feel free to email me. Please send a photo,of yourself and I will surely do the same.

age: 22

- do NOT contact me with unsolicited services or offers

HOE$

Silly hoes,

chase boys.

Dumb hoes,

talk noise.

Desperate hoes,

buy toys.

In denial hoes,

miss dolla$, walk past stacks and catch coins.

On this one again I clowns.

Why they all running?

Because T. Man's bitch, Lady Nikki

just dropped a penny on the ground.

I'm that bitch!

 here's a free hand me down!

By: K. Nicole Howard (October 17, 2014)

IT'S ALL GOOD UNTIL IT'S NOT!

Things between Montana and I were okay and getting better. I had almost mastered the hoe game and gotten good at being able to travel alone back and forth to Santa Barbara, which was only 4 hours away from Southeast San Diego. I could be sent and trusted to bring all the money back home to "Daddy". He didn't make me call him that but that was our situation. We were still on a first name and baby this-baby that situation-ship. I would also go to Las Vegas on the regular to visit friends and family. I couldn't be with them much because he knew those were my old stomping grounds. He could not risk me getting too far away from him and going against the grain. When I was in town of course, I made time for my girls Deez and Breezy along with dinner or lunch with Forever. I had finished all my DUI course online but still did all my driving with no L's, crazy I know but I always had a car before I had a license so, FUCK IT, I would get one eventually.

Montana heard about West Texas popping from a few of his pimp partners and decided it would be a good look for us since he only had 1 month left on paperwork. So, I played Santa Barbara until it was time to go. Our last visit there I was robbed at gun point by a trick. Per usual procedure Montana was downstairs sitting in the car of the Motel 8 parking lot. I let him know when it was good, I had the ends (money) and he hung up. The trick had been dressed in a costume, a full wig, two sets of clothes and everything. When he pulled the wig off and began to undress I was very uneasy and texted Montana the situation and told him to call and stay on the line with me, he did. It only took the guy about 3 - 4 minutes to ejaculate and he wasn't happy about that and had claimed he had been robbed because he paid for a 30-minute service but every nut after the first was an additional $150.00. The trick wasn't going for that, he pulled out his gun saying, "Well, since you're not willing to cooperate then take this bullet or I'm going to need a refund." I begged and pleaded with the man, "Please, whatever you do don't shoot me, I will get you your money and you can leave. Just don't kill me." Every inch of my being was shaking, I was loud enough so Montana could hear what was going on and could come to my aid. He was taking too long and I wasn't going to try and stall a man who had a loaded gun to my head. "You're waiting for your pimp huh? There's enough to go around sweetheart. GET ME MY MONEY!" the trick said. I ran to the bathroom and retrieved the money from underneath my shower bath mat and put it in his hand.

Without even counting it the trick ran out of the Motel 8 door, around the corner and hit the stairs, there was Montana chasing yet again another trick. My soul felt like it had been taken from my body. For a second time I realized I put my life on the line for this bullshit and this time, almost died for someone else's gain. When Montana made it back to me, he held me until I could stop my body from shaking, I was hysterical yet again. I had fallen asleep in his arms, when I woke Montana was still holding me tight. I got up showered and looked at the clock that read 3:05 A.M. I reposted my Backpage ads for all three of my phones and my got my head back in the game with *Problem's- The Separation* album blasting from the bathroom. Montana woke up, walked up behind me and held me closer than close. "Baby? You good? What you doing?" he asked. I replied, "I'm to this money, we leave for Texas in a few hours. It's still all money in, right? I asked. Montana smiled, lifted my body to the bathroom counter and loved my every curve before I began breaking these tricks. "You know I love you right, you are an amazing woman to me and my kids. My Mom adores you. She says she's never seen me smile so much in life until I met you. You gone be my wife Nikki, I mean that." Montana exclaimed looking so deep into my eyes, they instantly began to fill with water. I told him I loved him more before rushing him out the room because I had some money on the way and some more on my line. He reassured me he'd stay closer to the room just in case anything else, but my head couldn't dwell on the negativity or I'd fuck off the rest of the "rush hour", after the club money.

When I said, I loved him more that's exactly what I meant though. I didn't mean I loved him more than he loved me. I meant I loved him more than the bad days behind and ahead of us. I loved him more than any fight we would ever have. I loved him more than the distance I could feel beginning to cloud our relationship. I loved Montana more than any obstacle that could try and come between us. I loved him the most.

In loving him the most I got the least that I deserved from him and from myself.

I didn't know it then, but that was where the problems would begin. I had nothing to give myself, nothing to give to him either. Unbeknownst to me, that wasn't anywhere near the real definition of love.

We made it to Odessa, Texas in about 2 days, it was dusty, dry, and dirty as hell. The roads and highway were different from anything I had ever seen and the night life was trash. None of that mattered, I went there to party, get my money and up my regular clientel. After I accomplished all of that I would get ghost like I did every other state I had been to. I was at the top of my game though, nothing nor no one was bringing me down.

Montana knew I was loyal and had no intentions on going anywhere anytime soon no matter what we went through personally, I was rocking with the Piru 69, Bottum Boy from Southeast San Diego and everyone knew it. After being in Texas for about 2 months Montana and I had issues finding the things that we wanted and were a custom to having at our disposal. The pills, the weed, the Promethazine syrup. So, of course he knew some of everyone in the state of California. It wasn't long before a package was mailed to him. That 3 pounds was gone in about a two-week period, I was shocked and wanted nothing more for him and me than to double, triple and possible quadruple our earnings in half the time we had expected. Plus, that gave him his own lane to do his own thing instead of out here at these bitches and chilling with his struggling pimp homies who were claiming pimping but doing way more tricking and playing house with their hoes. Montana said to me one evening, "Baby, I got this plan right. If we can make $10,000.00, I'll go back to Diego and get what I need and come back. If it keeps booming like it did those two-weeks, we in there." I was convinced not only because I see how fast it moved but because no one else out here had the guts or plugs that he did to even bust a move like that. In two-weeks, I had made $20,000.00, he went came back and that was his thing.

He met a real loyal cat by the name of Windy from Chicago. He had a chick he met that was from Odessa, TX and knew how to move, her name was Cash. From that day forward the four of us were a team, not to be fucked with. We showed up at the functions lit and unknown. No one knew what hit them. It was crazy. I didn't function much because I was still on my hoe business and didn't care too much for the lime light or for too many people. My theory, keep a short list… be aware of the things that lived in tall grasses, SNAKES. When I was in town I would try to relax for a bit to no avail because then I would be a lazy, comfortable bitch and quite frankly I didn't want to hear that shit from Montana.

To change things up a little and to keep the heat off Montana and Windy, Cash and I would make the drive from West Texas to Southeast Diego to go get the packages and bring them back. Now, we not talking about small packages. This was real weight when you got both our niggas sending us on the road with $40,000.00/ a piece! Yeah, like that. We'd get into San Diego in the evening, rest up at a hotel, 8:00 A.M. bright and early, it was down to business and back on the road. Yes, two-day trip turnarounds but on the flip side we were taken care of and solid to a fault. Cash and I had gone on an official Molly pill diet, we had to stay awake and alert at all time. During this time, Cash and I had time to bond and establish a relationship.

Not only were our dudes hustling buddies but during this time both Cash and I were getting beat up on the regular. One week it was her eye, the next it was my arms, legs, or eye bruised up as well. Montana and I only had three or four physical altercations but that was still too many. I wouldn't wish a man's aggressive hands on any woman. No woman deserves that but it's what we put up with sometimes. I had no appetite because of the drug and would be sure to drown my body in orange juice, which did nothing for the fact that my body had gone from a solid Serena Williams stature to a frail Whitney Houston. I was sick and didn't even know it, at my lowest I weighed in at 115 pounds. I called it my Beyoncé stage but from the outside looking in I was dying, killing myself slowly. All the while I had bitches and 16 and 17-year-old broads hitting my Facebook talking this T. M. this and Montana that bullshit. I knew he was fucking around but with little girls, hell no bro'! That was gross.

One of the chicks I recruited to work for us. I needed someone to fill my spot. He flew her out to Texas and did some super big tricking. The girl liked me and only agreed to deal with me anyway but because it was not only my program but Montana's as well, I introduced them. Boy was that a mistake to introduce a nigga who ain't never had one bad bitch on his team, let alone two! The girl had been ignoring me and when I finally got her to pick up her line she laced me with nothing but facts. Told me about what my home looked like, what kind of car Montana was driving, what mall and club they had been to while she was in town those two days, not to include the fact that he paid for the round-trip airfare. I was livid!

Before hanging up with her to confront Montana I let her know, "Bitch, if you lying I have all your info and I'm bringing it to your front door." After hanging up with her I called Montana and cussed him out something serious. Of course, he denied every bit of it. After hanging up with me he texted the girl who then screenshot me all his text. He was mad that she would run her mouth, told her how good she could've had it but she couldn't wait for him to ditch me, I was again in tears and needed to go. Air was necessary if I planned on getting through this situation. I had a regular inn Corpus Christi, Texas named Job who was madly in love with me and that's where I went. Job was a sweet man who I met during one of my first trips to Corpus. It started off as a regular hoe/trick situation, but he taught me things. When I went to visit he'd pay me $6,000.00 for the whole weekend but most times there was no sex.

I had a *Porcha Cayenne* I had I had the keys to and he drove his turbocharged *Land Rover Sport.* Job was one of the biggest defense attorneys in his whole region and in the state of Texas. He taught me things about my body, mind and soul. We could really talk about life and didn't judge my situation but offered all the time to be my way out. He would say, "When you ready to come home to stay, you know home and I will be here. Your truck is missing you as I am." Job really cared for me and couldn't believe, understand or fathom why I was choosing this for my life. When I was with him I would drink some but I didn't need to. I didn't smoke any weed just my cigarettes and no pills were on the menu either. He had an in-home chef so I ate whatever, whenever, and however I'd like. This was a part of the game that was forbidden but Montana had been breaking the rules so me being more intelligent with bending them didn't faze me any.

I had talked to Job about how tired I was, how drained I was of the whole situation, out of the 3 ½ years of doing this I've never had a vacation. He was the first and only man I enjoyed being with other than Montana. I dreaded going back to Odessa, TX, I already knew what it was. Before I'd left I caught Montana in the trap fucking the bartender from a restaurant we were frequent customers at called *Cheddars.* Job fixed his mouth to say the most fulfilling words I had ever heard a man speak. He said, "If you could see what I see with my eyes, if you could taste how delicious you are with my mouth, if you felt the passion I feel with you, if you heard your moans with my ears you understand why I really need you here.

Nikki, leave and never look back, even if it's not with me you know I'll be here but he's going to kill you or you're going to kill yourself. Promise me you will be okay to go back and keep in touch with me after you leave this nigga man." I cried and promised to do just that. Before I laid down to make love to Job he prayed with me, in that prayer I asked God to show me if this relationship wasn't for me let me see and give me the strength to leave and never look back. I was tired, I was worn, hurt, just beat by it all and wanting nothing more than my family and a second chance that I knew only Christ can give to his child, HIS daughter.

Being able to empty out my soul before my flight back to Odessa, Texas was just what the doctor ordered. Once returning to Odessa, Texas Montana he had moved in two Hispanic girls in one of our apartments. One was supposed to 18-years-old and the other 19-years-old. He said we had business in California and wanted me to train them while he would return to Texas with his last package before our two-week vacation to the Bahamas. I was reluctant and completely over all his shenanigans, so I didn't care what went on with these girls, plus they had no identification. I could tell he was fucking one of them and even got us to do a threesome with him before he left back to Odessa, Texas.

Once he left it was all fun and games for them, I was working. The girls ended up fighting one another while I was driving from a date and all hell broke loose. The one he was fucking, his new pet project called him and he got on my line with the fuckery. "Nikki, what the fuck? You supposed to be training the bitches, how much money have they made, she said you been sleeping, they don't know how to post, I guess I gotta do it all myself. How the fuck I'm supposed to get you off your feet if you don't have money to replace your money." As he continued to go off, I could feel the steam blowing from my ears and water boiling from my head. Before he could call me anymore bitches, I went in.

I went completely off for the last time, "Montana, look, check this shit out. DON'T EVER DISRESPECT MY GANGSTA LIKE THAT. I BEEN RIDING WITH YOU AND YOU TAKE ANOTHER LIL'BITCH WORD FOR WHAT THE FUCK I GOT GOING ON. I DO MY OWN THING I DON'T NEED NO HELP AND NEVER TOOK ANY KIND OF BREAKS OR VACTIONS IN BETWEEN AND IN THE MEAN TIME.

IT'S BEEN ALMOST FOUR YEARS AND WE HAVE YET TO SEE ANY HUNGRY DAYS OR CASHLESS NIGHTs. YOU CAN HAVE THESE KIDS BACK AND ALL THE OTHERS YOU BEEN FUCKING ON. HAVE MY CAR PACKED WHEN I GET BACK, I'M DONE WITH THIS SHIT. I'M OUT, I'M BRINGING YOUR KIDS BACK TO YOU."

I packed my things, packed the two Hispanic girls and made my way to Los Angeles to empty out the storage unit that we had there because it was in my name before hitting the road back to Texas. I'd had it. He crossed the line too many times and I was done. In my head, I knew he would never be able to replace me but since he thought he could who was I to deny him a fair shot at trying. The whole drive back I cried, it was the most emotional, breaking point I ever had in my life. Montana was texting the Hispanic girl that was evidently my replacement but wasn't speaking to me at all. When I was 3 hours out from Odessa, our song came on and that was the last sign I needed to know, yup it was over. *Rick Ross ft. John Legends Who Do We Think We Are* played on repeat the whole way to my apartment. As I cried and sang, sang and cried I thought to myself, *Damn, that was supposed to be us.*

When I finally made it to the apartment and unpacked my car, Montana was sitting on the love sofa playing the game like he was the king of everything. I had been driving three straight days, Santa Barbara to Los Angeles, Los Angeles to Odessa and planned on leaving that night to Vegas. I packed my things and got my youngest brother Kris from one of the trap locations. Kris was having a hard time in Vegas getting a job so I told Montana since he was hitting the 40 Freeway on his way back to Odessa, after leaving me to do on the job training to these girls, pick up my brother and let him make a few ends, get some bread for a while until I returned. Then, I would help him find a job and get up for a little while in Texas.

Kris had only been there a week before the shit blew up and I had made up my mind to leave Montana for good. He had done well with the little time he was there and had been made aware of the reality of Montana and I's relationship but managed to out of it. I put as many of my things in garbage bags and stuffed them in my *2009 Cadillac CTS,* my dream car.

While packing the two girls were scared and expressed their need for me to stay. I told them I couldn't do it any longer. That if they wanted this nigga, they could have him. Pissed and all I still made them aware of the thing my aunt always told me.

"The same way you get him, will be the same way you lose him"

I was in a petty mood and had everything to prove so, since they wanted to leave so bad I told them to prove it. They had to show me. They were given two options; I will take you home or you can go to Vegas with me. They both packed a bag, crawled out the room window and met me in the car. Montana, still on the couch in front of the game…not one word exchanged between us. I smirked evilly, mashed on the gas to get Kris and before I could get there Lamont was on my line talking crazy. I didn't really want the little broads anyway but I had been in touch with another pimp or two who knew what to do with them once I got to Las Vegas. I knew they had no identification, so it wouldn't be too much for them to do, didn't make me any difference what they do.

Montana texted and called like crazy while we were on our way to Las Vegas. Between my phone and the Hispanic chicks, he blew up out lines. Because only one of my lines and her only line was in his name he went to *Verizon* and cut them off. I still had a burner phone and my own *T-Mobile* line he couldn't touch. The whole way to Las Vegas my youngest brother Kris couldn't believe what had just happened. "Nigga! You just gone run off with the nigga hoes like that? Yo' ass is crazy! See? Therefore, I can't mess with no black woman, you crazy for this one bro.", Kris said. I didn't take them because I wanted to, I didn't take them at all. They both seen what I had put up with and knew once I was gone it would be on them, they had two options, go home or to Vegas, they chose Vegas and I was petty.

I also had a point to make: If they will volunteer to go with your bottom bitch, ME. Who and what else would they do for a stranger, where's the loyalty, how strong is your pimping really? IT AINT PIMPING, MONTANA HAD BEEN PLAYING HOUSE! Exactly two days after I had gotten to Vegas, Montana was right behind me. He got the broads and my Cadillac back, I was done with him anyway.

I made my point, made him waste time and money, best of all had done him the same way he'd done me. I was satisfied. Montana ended up getting a place out in Las Vegas, played house with his broads and still lightweight functioned in Texas.

In October 2013, I found out I was 8 weeks pregnant. Just when I thought I was rid of this nigga I find out I'm stuck with him for the remainder of this human life. If not him physically, the child I was bearing would have his blood running warm through their veins. We were on speaking terms off and on so I knew things were progressively getting worse with him. Montana has gotten caught a few times and was expected to turn himself in September 2014 but before then he decided to take one last run to Odessa, Texas. That indeed was his last run. He stayed with me the whole month of July, our son Logan Love Moore was born July 11, 2014 and Montana got caught up in Arizona on his way to Texas. Back to prison he went and that's where he would be for the next 3 ½ years. He didn't leave without the grand finale though because soon after that I found out that the Hispanic chick he was pimping on was due to have his daughter in September 2014. I'd promised myself that was the last time I'd let him hurt me. I was numb to it all. DONE.

Nikki,
   I hope this letter reaches you and Logan in the best physical and mental health. I'm going to start this letter where our phone conversation left off. First off I want you to know I love you! It's hard for me to express myself sometimes but this I know for sure. When you ask what I want to do or what I want from you I'm still confused. I want to be a everyday father for my son I know that for sure. My father just passed on the way our relationship was, the way I grew up and how he died I want to break that cycle! Logan is the first and only child I was their for birth. When I first held him I felt like a real man for the first time in life. This is the son I always wanted the apple of my eye! M or me!
The flip side to all this joy is reality! The reality is I can't have things my way, I made to many bad decisions an involved to many people. I'll be the first to admit I lost sight of the goal WE had! I never lost my love for you though but the money, drugs and

women did cloud my mind and confuse me. I'm only a man an it's happened to some of the best of them. Reality is I got another baby on the way as well an I want to be there for her too. These are the pros and cons to my situation Nikki: You were there when I had nothing helped me build what I had and was as ride or die as ride or die gets when we were together. When you left everything crumbled for me but while I was spiraling down Marisa was there picking up the slack and got pregnant. WOW Now the dilemma is who to choose, when neither one of you should suffer because I'm 100% to blame and I feel like shit about this because yall don't deserve this so yall are somewhat faultless and just got caught up in a tangled web called Lamar. I thought before I did my time I could some how smooth everything out but things never work out like that for me. I've been in a deep depression with no one to confide in. Like you said

to make each other happy I don't know
how it deteriorated but I want that back
The only reason I suggested y'all come toget
was because y'all were cool enough to leave
me together an my selfish mind wanted to
be able to be at home with both of
my kids sorry for only thinking of myself.
I honestly want to know how you feel th
can work out without the kids taking
a loss? I don't have all the answers
Nikki can you imagine where my mind is
right now? I've been driving myself crazy
over this for awhile now and sometime
I just want to give up. I dug my own
grave type shit. You know how I feel
about my kids I'll do whatever I can
to better there lives. As I sit here
withering away I deserve whatever comes
to me. I wish someone taught me how
to be a man or taught me how to
stand for something. I wasn't blessed
with a loving family mother and fath
or anything nobody to teach me about th
world I only learned from my own mistak

send me pictures of Logan I would appreciate it. This my only paper and envelope so as soon as I get more I'll write again.

P.S.
Sorry so sloppy we're on lockdown and the pencil about a inch long. which is no excuse. From me to you though its way harder then it looks keeping a straight face when you come from absolutely nothing it changes alot of things. I can't say what type of person I'll be when I get out I just know I'll be stronger and colder. I know I ain't shit and you and Logan deserve better so whatever you choose to do you have my blessing. I wont be gone to long but I feel it's over for me. I know it'll take alot of love and help to get me back right and people don't give that anymore so Lord knows what's in store for my future. Don't feel any sorrow it is what it is. Hopefully I'll hear from you. Tell my son I love him dearly an I wish with all my heart I could be there for him an if I have the opportunity to teach him the things I had to learn on my own I would love to. Well its back to the jail time. I love you

LOVE ME, MY LOVE

Love me unconditionally,

Love me faithfully,

Love me my love.

Love me sincerely,

Love me consistently,

Love me my love.

Love me deeply,

Love me joyfully,

Love me my love.

Love me generously,

Love me passionately,

Love me my love.

Love me forever,

Love me always,

Love me my love.

For it is only your love.

By: K. Nicole Howard - February 17th, 2017

THIRD OF THREE

The date is March 30, 2017, still following the three loves in a lifetime theory, the third love I never seen coming. This is the one that looks all wrong for us and that destroys any lingering ideals we cling on to about what love is supposed to be. This is the love that comes so easy it doesn't seem possible. It's the kind where the connection can't be explained and knocks us off our feet because we never planned for it. This love came from Kristin learning to love self. Once I figured out what "self" meant I started falling deeply in love with ME. The true 'self' is love, and nothing but love. I am at peace with "self" as well as in harmony with others.

People will go to great lengths to achieve another's love, when they are the epitome of love.

Even though we have the power to heal our self, we also have the power to stop what we want to happen, from happening when we refuse to forgive, holding on to anger and resentment without healing. Being present with oneself in ways that honor and respect the divine within inspires greater awareness and maturity. When you choose to live life as a victim, blaming others for misfortunes, not willing to forgive or trust your inner instinct urging you to do so, it is because you are out of touch. You are refusing to accept your authentic self. Being in touch with my authentic self means I started to listen to my inner voice calling me back to a place of familiarity where peace, love and compassion resides. This place I am being called to is constantly informing me to do what makes me feel better; whole and complete. Not focusing on what has happened to me, but informing myself to let go of anything that makes us feel uneasy.

Now, I currently reside in a place of acceptance, realizing that all of life's experiences have value, meaning and purpose. That my life has helped me to find ways to take effective action, redirecting my language and conversations in ways that will help me to thrive, and explore other options. The ultimate goal is to strive to be well, so I, Kristin can better serve self and others. This being most important during challenging times, similar to the ones I have shared with you in this book, my story.

Life is a journey of self-discovery, self-examination and self-realization. Until there is an outward response to an inner awakening nothing will change. It is the happenings inside of me that caused shifts in the outer experiences I encounter every day. I am a completely sober, mother of a 2 ½ year old son; Logan Love Moore. Not too much longer after my sons' birth I began my loc' journey and decided to **TRUST THE PROCESS!** I drink socially but not out of necessity. I have reestablished my relationship with Christ and my family. I am in a better place. I have relocated back to my hometown, Arizona and starting my new career as a school teacher.

Although I wasn't thrilled about being a single mother it has been the most rewarding experience life has had to offer me. My son has taught me to live life as he does, everything is an adventure. Life has new unknown territories that need exploring. I am perusing my Master's degree in clinical psychology and have my life experiences to thank for that. My son's dad and I are in contact and on speaking terms, he is due to be released this year and co-parenting is the plan. The dating scene has been fun but I'm still in the healing process and don't want to jump the gun too soon. I've grown to enjoy my own company.

I said all this to say, NEVER LOSE HOPE AND FAITH IN GOD. It is not because any of my own doing that I survived all this, God brought me through every step of the way. It is not by chance or coincidence that I wasn't murder, missing, or overdosed on drugs. Nowadays it's the new fad. It's the new cool to be so called, "trappin". That's not the only thing out here and at the end of the day it's only so many problems that money can fix.

You can't put a price on living a productive and successful life.

I remember days that I prayed for the inner peace that I now have today. I had to learn how to love me first. I would never forget the dark reality of my past. This taught me a lesson that there is always something to learn. Now I can believe anything is possible. Your dedication to make it possible along with the love and support of family and friends who have your best interest at heart is what we really need. I have every reason to be bitter, ugly and ungrateful but no, I'm choosing ***LOVE*** every time!

Sunday, 13 June 04

Dear ~~█████~~,

I could not write until I prayed about what I should and should not say.

I'm going to speak to you as a young lady, not so much as my daughter. Keep this letter as you will probably need to refer back to it at various times.

First you must know and come to understand the talents and gifts you have been given. Second you <u>must</u> see that you have a real enemy, who <u>does not</u> want you to become any of the things God has in store for you. Good for you that it is not up to the enemy, but up to you as to how far you go.

As you grow into a young lady you will need to learn how to tell <u>your flesh</u> NO! and mean it. If you don't you will never be able to complete anything because your emotions and your body will run you, instead of your/God's spirit being in control.

Guys will be guys and they will seldom change. Just as I told Precious you must <u>never</u>

—2—

build your life around any man. He should not control your thoughts and you should always have a choice in any matter. Once you allow him to tell you to come and go you are just another "toy".

I can't tell you how proud of the work you have done writing and taking care of yourself as a young lady. But you still have so much more room to grow.

Honors will be a challenge for you, but not impossible. In Prov. 23:7a ..."as he thinketh in his heart, so is he":

The additional issue with your's keep breaking the rules are that no one can trust you and its not fair to the people who are staying or trying to stay out of trouble. You keep getting chances and they aren't getting in trouble. It causes a hard time for everyone. Whether you live w/ your Grandmother or us.

If you intend on having any length of life you must be obedient and respectful. If you don't you are causing your life to be shortened. As much as I love you it remains your choice.

(over→)

you should apologize your grandmother! And even when you don't agree it's regrettable to stay out of trouble and say O.K. Pray — You know how!

There was something that was said at Kenny's graduation. "You reach for the moon if you miss you still are amongst the stars."

Aim high as you can. Even if you don't get the moon at least you know you tried and didn't just take the easy way and you put your best foot forward. You reached for the hardest goal.

How do you know what's there if you don't push. You accomplish your goals with prayer and by taking one day at a time.

Phil. 4:13 "I can do all things through Christ which strengtheneth me."

Love
always,

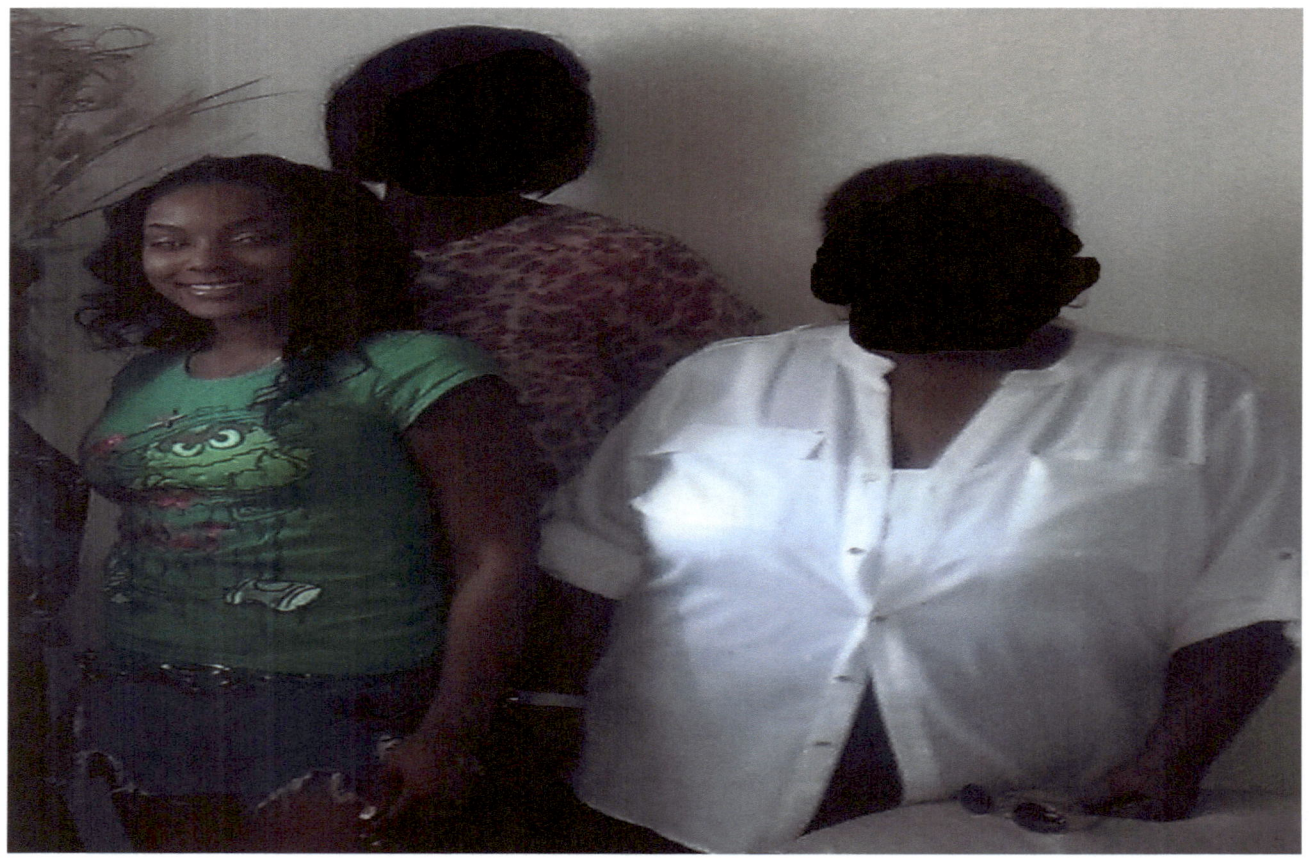

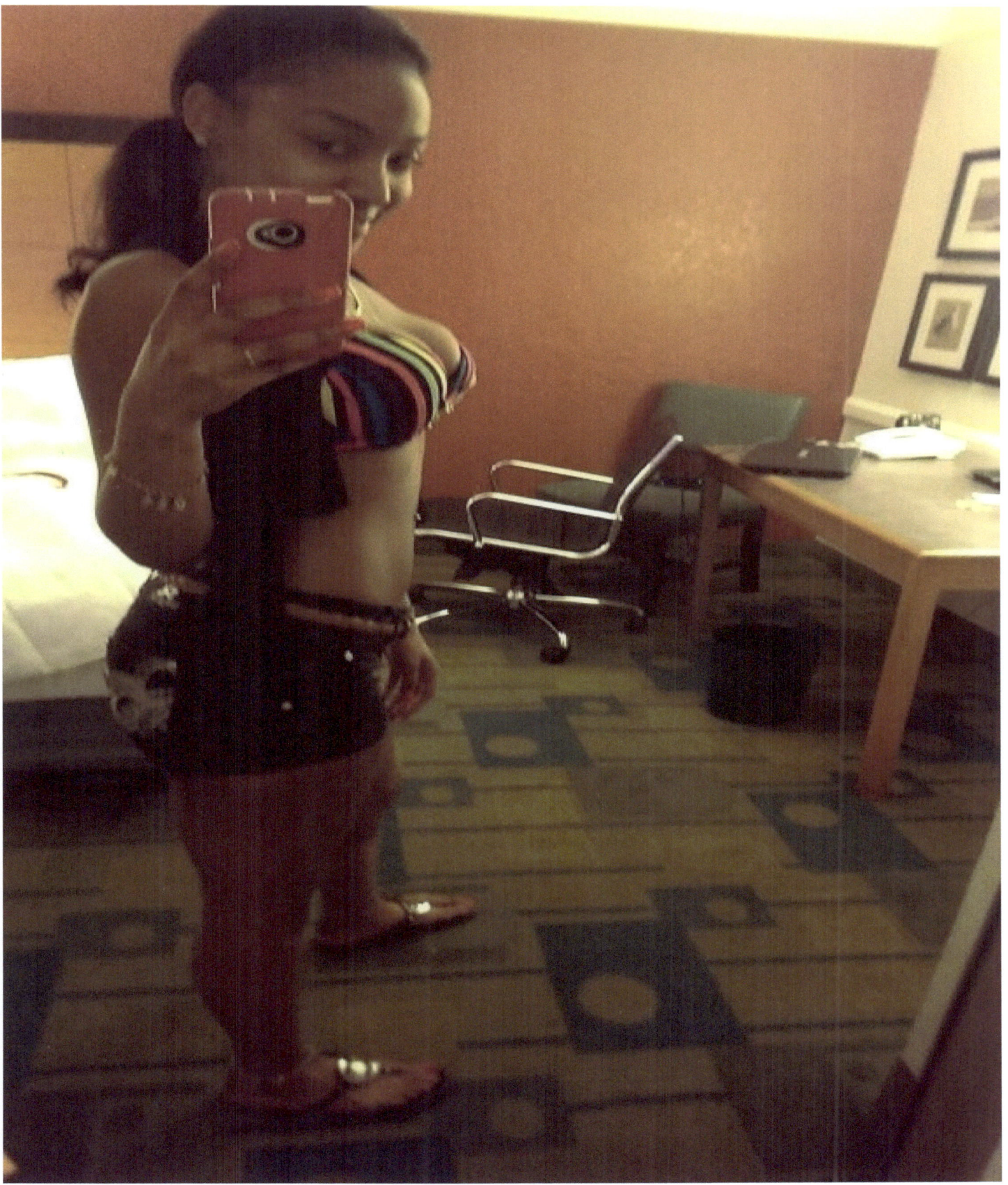

Nov 19, 2013 at 9:05pm

Ike Turner and Tina Turner is just like Mike Tyson and Cus D'Amato with out the right push wether it be ass whoopin or stamina training with the right nigga with you giving you that drive that motivation that ambition them goals! Bitch you wouldnt be shit I turn you up an on who! Mantana thats who! Ohhhh yeeeaaaah! (In my Randy Savage voice)

 and 6 others

👍 Like   💬 Comment   ➤ Share

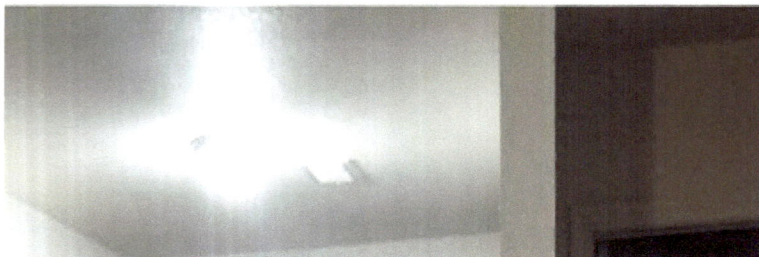
Nov 19, 2013 at 5:47pm

I aint had to cook for myself in months but I still got it tho lol! #NoFilter #NoBitch #FoodPorn #MarieCalender #Microwavable #CantCook

Nov 23, 2013 at 11:18am

Nigga knock me for the bottom dont serve me kidnap my other broads an wonder why they back with me. Lets keep it P got all the bitches back weirdo! Mantana aka Still-On youve been served kidnapper. Had one of my cars an everything. Pull up 1000 miles away knock my bitches back an leave walking scary nigga back to the money counting machine. Now me an my nephew finna tear up the Versace store. Like a Pimp should tho. Praise be to Allah oh an the nigga name Q or wayne some shit then pimpin turn around an make my bottom stay you aint gotta stay here but you aint leaving with me! Boom left the duck now its swans all in my pond. No more locked doors and no more black bitches! Viva la raza bitch!

👍 Like   💬 Comment   ➤ Share

👍 You, 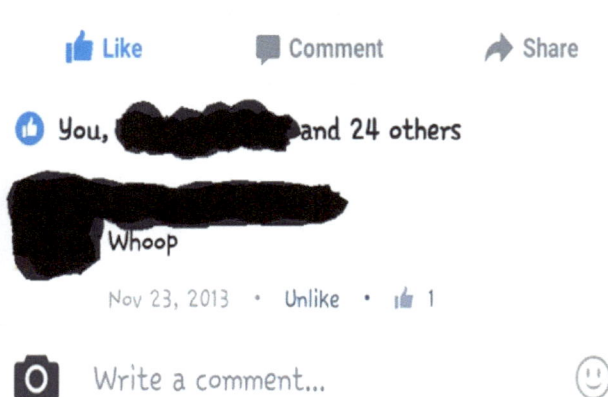 and 24 others

Whoop
Nov 23, 2013 • Unlike • 👍 1

📷 Write a comment...   ☺

Nov 1, 2013 at 9:43am

On mamas today a bitch gone get fired an out my life for good

👍 and 14 others   3 Comments

👍 Like   💬 Comment   ➤ Share

TO BE CONTINUED…

#*IAMMYSISTERS*